American Druthers

~ Michael McNaney ~

Written specifically for...

Those that use guns as a tool
Those who collect guns
Those that don't want anything to do with guns
Those who make their living from guns
Those that make their living using guns
Those that hunt with guns
Those who are highly trained to use guns
Those who have used guns to protect life
Those who have lived after being shot by a gun
Those whose hobby or sport is shooting guns
Those who threaten with guns
Those that feel threatened by guns
Those that horde guns
Those that carry a gun exposed
Those that carry a gun concealed
Those that are afraid of guns
Those that are obsessed with guns
Those that don't know what to think about guns

...All Americans

With Love, and Hope for a better future, this book is dedicated to the families and friends of those killed or maimed in U.S. Sanctioned Gun Violence within the borders of our Free American Society.

CONTENTS

Foreword by the Author

I wish I were somewhere else. I wish there were no need. I wish my mind would rest... But, I'm not, there really is, and it won't.

These are all Druthers. "I would rather," is what druthers means. It is a squish of three words that I first heard of in the tales of Tom Sawyer and Huckleberry Finn. It's a lazy mouth way of getting to the end of a sentence, yet still conveying the intent of the sentence. It is a colloquialism of middle America lightly used when thinking back on situations that we wish were different. Like everyone reading this, there are a lot of things in my life and my surroundings that I wish were different.

I'druther things were different but they aren't.

Although I am more than sure readers on both sides of our shiny American coin would prefer this book validate their personal feelings on firearms, this book is neither Anti-Gun nor Pro-Gun. There are quite a few of those books, I certainly wouldn't wish to add to that number. This book has been written and edited to be entirely Pro-American and Pro-human. Through these chapters I hope to emphasize the sage and thought provoked ideals of ;

- We Hold These Truths to be Self-Evident -
- All Men are Created Equal -
and
- Life, Liberty and the Pursuit of Happiness -

At first glance, angles presented here may seem tinged to the political left, yet the political left will most likely think I'm an insidious conservative. But no, I'm not taking a stance other than to say that at some level we can actually have both our cake, and eat it too. We can have responsible gun ownership in America and public safety at the same time. This book is not about railing against other people's political ideas, it is about you, your family and our neighbors. We are the ones with the need for personal protection and we are also the ones dying at random in large numbers.

- FOREWORD -

Other than to stand on this soap box, this issue is no longer about me. I have already been taken out of this situation. I have come to the end of my personal firearms chain and am quite content with myself. This is about an American feeling of solidarity in Patriotism for the American way of life and how to better move towards that nearly forgotten feeling.
Here in this book, I am trying to offer something different to think about in relation to the standard American firearms issue.

This book is also a type of autobiography and hopefully at the same time a thought-provoking essay presented to be used as parable and example for those with the ability to take any positive meaning. The snippets of biography explore an average American life. A life growing up with and living with firearms, and the events that have happened in relation.

Written from the perspective of a highly trained, gun owning and otherwise "everyday" American, I hope to add an editorial view from a side that is rarely heard from and is generally missing from the modern firearms discussion - *the victim's point of view.* There are alternate angles of thought and points of view for every single subject imaginable and the more angles we are aware of, the better our decision-making process can be. A little understanding can go a long way. I hope to be able to emphasize this isn't about the tool, it is about the people using that tool. The use of this tool being merely a symptom of our increasingly abhorrent American condition.

Another thing to note before you read this book is that I am not a professional writer, and certainly not an aspiring "Author." What I am is an American that has been touched by one of the most pressing topics we as Americans face in our daily lives, someone with a deep insight urged forward by the end of life. Although I have written a few published articles and journaled a trip or two, my knowledge and patience with strict literary structure is short, so please bear this in mind.

I am sure that those interested in this topic will find this read eye opening, others will find it interesting, and I expect many people heavily invested in this subject will vilify my reasoning.

In these pages I will show how, with thought and respectful responsibility, we can cut our horrific yearly shooting numbers to a small percentage of current levels. We can have guns in our modern American society and we can also have public safety. My goal here in these pages is to present reason to thought, example to need and truth to consequence. Presenting real life situation to spurn thought and exploration of possible solutions to the paranoia and indignant attitudes at work within todays issues on gun ownership and use in the United States.

Thank You, for taking time out of your life to read this book.

American Druthers

- Love Story Gone Bad -

So how does one go about writing a book about guns in America without taking sides? How can I convey my experience, thoughts and ideas on responsible gun ownership and tolerance of others, without the waitress spitting in my soup, or having to slink around and take the back alleys home?

Over the last few years, I have asked this question to several people, but the answers always seem to come from one political side or the other, with little digs thrown in for good measure. The problem with those answers is, that writing a book about guns in America from a political view is either preaching to the choir on one end, or inciting a riot on the other, there is no equal ground there. Those angles haven't worked in the past and I doubt they ever will. But still, I don't need any more enemies, especially gun owners, and I don't think I can live the rest of my life hesitant of my Starbuck's latte'.

After quite a bit of back-and-forth, the answer I finally came to was honest and most personal. *Tell it like it is;*

I have a Love / Hate relationship with guns.

That should do it, it covers both sides of the discussion and I just may be the perfect guy to tell the story.

As far as right now is concerned, guns don't bother me, it's some of the people using them wrongly that I have an issue with. But when I was young, I *loved* guns, I couldn't wait to be old enough to have one of my own. From a very young age, I've been blessed with an unusual aptitude for mechanical devices. Firearms are just that, they are precision mechanical devices.

So, when I discovered them, I was enthralled.

I guess you could say that I was exposed to the American obsession for guns early in my life. Not as deeply engrained in my mind as some people, and I wasn't exposed to them at a *very* young age as some people have been, but in that fact perhaps lies my basis for moderation with firearms. Throughout my life the attitude in my family concerning guns was never extreme. Guns were never revered, or talked about much at all, they were just another part of life. My parents were average mid-western, mid-twentieth century types striving for the available comforts offered in those years. They didn't have me pulling triggers or cleaning guns at five years old, or dress me in camouflage as I grew up, but I still developed an itch. A red blooded American, blue steel itch. I didn't know that guns and the way they are being used throughout our society is a uniquely American issue. I didn't know that there was a controversy surrounding firearms. I just knew I liked the mechanical aspects of guns and that they made a great noise and resulted in destruction. What could be better? These are the things that initially attracted my attention. The same reasons most youngsters are attracted to guns, mechanics, noise and destruction.

My earliest recollection involving a gun that I can completely remember is going hunting with my Father when I was too young to even use one. I can't place the age, maybe seven or eight years old. I remember it was just the two of us and the gun being very loud.

[*Side Note:*
I personally think that children of ten years and under should be left to children's things. Guns are certainly not toys, and children this young, do not yet have the mental capacity, or even dexterity, to take on a killing device.]

Anyway... I can remember my Father and I walking through the woods somewhere in Iowa. He, carrying his 20-gauge Winchester pump action shotgun, wearing a purpose-made canvas hunting jacket.

2 ~

And me, watching intently as we scouted squirrels in the trees to shoot. He did shoot a couple but we didn't keep them. We've never specifically talked about it, but I imagine he took me out there for an introduction to the noise and skills of hunting.

It was also at around seven or eight years old when some friends and myself were playing in the woods not too far from home and found a clean and loaded lever-action .22 caliber rifle.

Somehow without playing with it or hurting ourselves, we got it back to my house where my Mother called the police to come pick it up. I imagined it being dropped by burglars as they made their getaway from robbing a house. At that age I'm sure that idea was a result of suggestion overheard from adults, but to this day, that's actually the only plausible reason I can think of for such a find. I mean, how else could it have possibly appeared there lying on the ground unattended in the woods?

It's harder to fully remember things from a very young age, but some things stand out. Occasionally events pop into my head that I haven't thought of in decades...

I have an Uncle, my Mothers brother, that is only four years older than myself. Because of this small age difference, when we were both young, he was charged with watching me and keeping me out of trouble when we visited. Of course, as you might imagine, this was not a favorite pastime of his. Once, when I was nine or ten we were visiting and I was tagging along as always. We were out playing in the woods with a group of his friends and I was along for the day. I don't remember the exact circumstance, but while we were playing with BB guns in the woods with his friends, I was the only one that didn't have a real BB gun and was a convenient ragging post for the much more "mature" youngsters. A standard situation for kids throughout the ages. At that age, these small age differences matter, and being so much younger than them all, one of the boys was relentlessly picking on me. So much so, that after a while I was getting tired of it.

Soon, we crossed a stream and I was asked to hold a gun for one of them as they crossed. As I remember, something upsetting was said to me, I turned red, and mouthy got shot in the rear with a pump action Crossman, which ended in him doing a slo-mo into the water. The memory is a blur from there, so I must not have bled in retribution or punishment.

At the ages from eight to twelve my Father and I went hunting several times with my Grandfather and that same Uncle at a place called the Christian Center, in the middle of Iowa. I remember walking the fields along with the grown-ups on pheasant and quail hunting weekends. I wasn't allowed a gun but I paid strict attention to every nuance of the hunting custom.

A small side note being that nobody ever accidentally got shot in the face as far as I can remember.
Do you remember that? If not, look this one up.
Our dear old ex-Vice President and former top-secret squirrel Dick Cheney made a great example of himself for us. I consider him proof that in depth knowledge of gun safety is important even at the highest levels.
This was a man charged with leading our country, sending our young ones off to kill and die, and himself not having the firearms skills needed to hunt quail. His example starting with "Accidents can happen to anyone," and ending with "Just keep the guns away from this guy," on the other. He has made a great example of himself on many fronts.

At one time, this next snippet was at the very top of the list for gun experiences in my life gone bad. I was eleven years old and my family was visiting friends of my parents, the house of a manager co-worker that my Father respected. I had been playing with others in the house as children do, and spotted a small semi-automatic pistol lying on a dresser unattended. I had never seen one of these before, and immediately catching my eye, I soon had it out of its holster curiously inspecting the piece.

I was mesmerized standing in front of the bedroom window looking at the gun when I heard my Mom calling my name.

With no time to put it back where I found it across the room, I quickly hid it away in my pants as to not get caught. Unfortunately, my Mother was coming to find me for the return trip home and I was ushered outside to the car before I could put it back where I found it. The car trip home was torturous, and we weren't home ten minutes before the phone was answered and the search began. Needless to say, everyone was in a terrible lather and the gun was soon found. That incident didn't turn out well, not well at all. A few short hours later I was in the hospital. Not from the gun itself but from the beat down I got from my Father when he found I was the one who had taken it. In retrospect of that event, if that would have happened with my son and myself in the same manner, I would have handled the situation a bit differently and also probably would have had one less friend. After-all, leaving a loaded pistol lying out in the open with a house full of young children is not very smart from any angle of excuse.

At eleven or twelve I was finally old enough to use a rifle for hunting. On hunting excursions, I was given the family heirloom, .22 single shot rifle to use. A popular child's rifle in its day, the Stevens Arms "Crack-shot" .22 caliber, two-piece rifle was a fine chunk of junk, at least this one was. I've heard many people wax nostalgic over their beloved first rifle, and many were a version of this little pea shooter. From the very first day till later when I was a teen, the only thing I was ever able to consistently hit with that gun were rats in a barn from ten feet away. Close range while bracing off the back of an old chair. The rats would poke their heads out of their hole in the side of the barn to see what was going on outside, just to find a reason to run. I was able to kill as many as I had patience for on a lazy South Georgia summer day. But that jumps ahead...

At the same ages of eleven and twelve I often played with my father's guns when no one else was home, they were put away but never locked.

One time, when playing with my father's shotgun, I cut open a few shotgun shells and removed the shot pellets. I then proceeded to chase my younger brother around the basement with the shotgun shooting him with hot wadding.

It wasn't as easy as all that of course, he jumped all over and I missed him quite a bit. But point being, it was dangerous, done stupidly long ago as a youth, and still a little funny as I think of it. How bent is that?

In those years the little .22 "Crack Shot" rifle broke a few flowerpots under other-than-legal circumstance also.

One time, I took it to a friend's house to brag and show him the dinky firearm. The rifle was easy to transport since it broke down in two pieces and fit in its own little canvas bag, but I ended up staying there too long. On the way home I was afraid my father might already be there when I stepped through the door, so I stashed it away in an evergreen cluster down the street to retrieve and replace the next day. It turned out, that later in the evening while looking for something in the basement, he somehow noticed it gone, and in the middle of the night I was abruptly woke from sleep to explain the missing gun.

Not too long after I turned sixteen, I used the birthday money I had been gifted and went to Kmart to buy a single shot, 16-gauge shotgun of my own to hunt and play with. At that time, my family lived in South Georgia, and in the South, a boy's 16th birthday nearly always included a gun as far as I ever knew. It was a rite of passage that a lot of folks observed since sixteen is the legal age for shotgun purchases in many states. That gun served me well to both hone my hunting skills and play with, but after a year or so, it ended up sawed off, both barrel and stock, to shoot like a pistol and blast things with.

It would still knock a squirrel off a tree branch from thirty feet away, but was specifically illegal to own being modified in such a way. In later years it was destroyed with a hammer out of spite after a seedy "friend" of mine tried to steal it. I don't quite remember why I crunched it instead of him, but it's enough to note that this particular gun is out of circulation.

I have found over my lifetime that there are some people in America that have a strange attraction to illegal firearms and extreme or illegal gun parts such as sawed-off shotguns, silencers, high capacity magazines, bump stocks etc. It is a different level of thought, a level of American owners that heed few gun laws no matter what the intent. A type of bad boy, "Don't Tread On Me," mentality.

Soon after buying the shotgun, probably at around seventeen years old, I saw a .30 caliber M1 carbine rifle on the wall at Kmart and had to have it. It was the same kind I'd seen in the World War Two movies that I liked. To make it more realistic, (to the movies I'd seen) I also purchased two thirty-round ammunition clips for it and had them taped together with duct tape, commando style for a quick sixty round capability.

That was a very accurate rifle.

I used to see how many cones I could shoot off a pine tree in a row without missing. I don't remember the exact number hit in a row, but it was quite high, over twenty for sure. I was quite proud of this accomplishment but admittedly, no thought was given as to what was behind those cones as the bullets whizzed through them, through the tree, and off into oblivion.

These years, my mid to late teen years, were full of hunting and screwing off with guns. As I mentioned earlier, at that time my family lived in South Georgia. In those parts, guns were in the rotation for things to do when you were bored.

One time when I was about 17 years old, I was at a friend's house during the summer months and we were looking for something to do.

My friend went into his father's closet and pulled out his Dad's new Savage, 7mm hunting rifle. Soon, we were in the back yard setting up targets to shoot. His yard was in the country and about an acre in size. I was surprised at the kick of the rifle and as we discussed it, my friend shot things in directions other than where we had set up the targets. Two days later I was at home, when the phone rang. I intercepted a call from his Father to my parents. When he found out it was me that picked up the phone, he lit into me right away. It turned out that one of his neighbors was forced to put down a cow since it had a bullet hole in a front leg and could no longer stand. My friend had inadvertently hit the cow from an unseen distance while shooting aimlessly that day. That cow was at least half a mile away when the bullet hit it. The neighbor that owned the cow had heard the gunfire that day and was calling around to ask if anyone knew anything. My friend's Dad didn't know anything to say right then, but he suspected, and checked his new rifle. He of course found cartridges missing and that the rifle had been shot and not properly cleaned.

I don't remember the outcome of that exactly but it was agreed that I wasn't the shooter. I *do* remember that I was banned from my friend's house from that point on.

Sometimes a different friend of mine and myself would go hunting all day and end up with a sack full of critters. At the end of the hunt, we could sell every one of them for $1 a piece to share croppers in the many "shotgun," country towns that dot that part of the state. We shot wood ducks for their feathers to make hatbands. We shot Fox Squirrels because we weren't supposed to. I even had a friend with a rare and endangered Black Squirrel taxidermized and mounted as a trophy to a small log in his den. We blasted mailboxes and signs as we careened down country roads, spot hunted deer at night, baited sink holes in the woods for ducks. We'd sight in scopes on a .22 rifle and indiscriminately pop the heads off birds at fifty yards.

These and many other forgettable instances that I am now completely embarrassed to have done.

Sounds deplorable doesn't it? Even depraved maybe, but guess what, that's the rule of the matter, not the exception. I'm merely one of the few that will admit to it. I didn't do much of it alone, and I can guarantee you, the same is going on at this very moment all over the Country.

I Positively Guarantee it.

A small bit of proof open for everyone to see being that nearly every road sign in rural America has bullet holes and shotgun blasts through them. A new road sign in the country has maybe a week before it gets ventilated. In my youth, my friends and I "swiss-cheesed," quite a few signs.

As you may have already guessed, when I was young, I was a hellion. Many of my friends' parents were wary of me. They imagined that I was a bad influence on their kids and conversely my parents thought the same of theirs. The truth was that we were all wild children with no attention paid to us, or direction to go. But what can you do, eh? Only one time in my adventures with guns was there ill intent with a gun. Any and all other times, the propensity for death and destruction was there, but we all had enough back woods "smarts," to avoid serious trouble.

Did your parents ever threaten to send you off to the orphanage when you were young? Mine never threatened, it just turned out that way. One time when my father thought he'd had enough, he wouldn't let me back in the house. I was too young to roam alone so I was sent for a stint at the local orphanage.

There was an alarm that rang in my head about that time, I woke up to the world just a little. I do not recommend sending your children to the orphanage. There were kids there that put my wild child practices to shame. My closest confidant there was a mild-mannered kid. I think I glommed to him because he seemed to not have the character to overshadow my own, and he to me, merely because I was the closest he'd known to freedom in quite a while. I hadn't been there very long when the two of us took off on a secret trip to his last foster home across town.

We found the doors locked, but he knew how to get inside and we soon raided the fridge and sat around talking of his "good old days." He obviously didn't like his father but I don't remember what that was for. I do remember him retrieving a loaded .38 revolver from somewhere in the house and pretending to draw a bead on his father's head as he pretended to pull the trigger several times. That pistol left with us and when we got back to the orphanage, I insisted on hiding it myself, then loosely "hid" it to be found. I'm pretty sure that me being kicked out of the orphanage for this offense was what saved his father's life. That kid had a blank twinkle in his eye that I've since seen only in dangerous people that are not correctly packaged. Later in life, that look was in the eyes of the guy that attacked me.

It'd be interesting to know where that kid's life went from there.

Along the way, and some time after that, I had a friend in the early 1980's that was booted out of the U.S. Army and somehow returned to his family salvage yard with a case of high explosive primers (blasting caps). I don't remember for sure but probably the very reason he was booted out of the Army in the first place. (does anyone remember the blasting cap danger commercials on TV in the 1970's?)

A couple properly sized iron pipes sunk loosely into the ground a foot or so deep acted as mortars. We used the primers, a 12v battery and driveshaft u-joint caps as our projectiles to hone in on anything and everything within range. We got pretty good too, eventually riddling an old school bus in the salvage yard with dozens of dents from flying u-joint caps. No telling what else was destroyed along the way, some of them "never came down."

Not a harrowing experience, but more of a tale of fun-and-games, there was a time when a couple friends and I would saddle horses and spend the afternoons playing cowboys and Indians.

We would bring our own bullets then easily slip the lock on the gun cabinet and use his family's guns, then go chasing "Indian" rabbits in a huge meadow on horseback. The grass was maybe a foot high and a safe haven for rabbits. There were dozens of burrows in this meadow. It was an afternoon of wack-a-mole as they bounced all over the place. The rabbits were terrified, but truth be-told, if we were riding around shooting, they were in absolutely no danger. We were using .22 caliber ten shot revolvers and .22 lever action rifles. I don't remember any of us ever hitting anything we shot at on horseback. I guess it's just too bumpy of a ride for the average adolescent rabbit blaster.

Throughout my time in South Georgia and North Florida, which lasted until I was around nineteen, everyone I knew owned guns. We all played with guns like they were regular toys. There were many, many fights and a knife was pulled once as I remember, but not once was anyone ever threatened or shot with a gun that I knew of... except one time, while at an illegal party in an illegal place, doing illegal things, I did have an opportunity thrust upon me to use a gun in defense.

This particular party area in the woods afforded enough space that different factions of rednecks could have their own bonfires and music and not bother each other. At those times, in one Saturday night there may be four or five different parties going on in the woods within a twenty to thirty-acre area.

Bikers, Street Racers, Stoners, KKK... you name the horde of vice and they were down there in the woods near the old steel bridge inebriated and waiting for "Free Bird" to make the rotation on a wailing car radio.

One of these Saturday evenings I was asked to take a girl home who was drunk and late for curfew. When I returned forty-five minutes later, the friend I came to the party with was being beat up and cut with a knife next to the campfire. I could see that guns were present.

I could see my friend on the ground with someone standing over him holding a knife to his neck and I could see blood on his clothes. Everyone else that was there with us previously was now gone, and in their place was a large group of long haired scruffy types drunkenly mulling around, urging on this one-sided attack.

When I saw what was going on with my friend, I quickly ran back to the truck and retrieved my M1 carbine rifle from the gun rack behind the bench seat.

A specifically illegal place to keep it, by-the-way.

Spraying bullets in the air and riddling their escape vehicles, I was able to disperse the assault, not get hit by returned pistol fire and get my friend to the hospital before he bled out from a knife wound to the neck. I seem to remember finding out later that it was a biker gang that did the deed, and in biker fashion, retribution was at first considered with high explosives that were available at that time for use. This put me very deep into a situation I was not comfortable in, it was going too far. There was a choice to be made so I took the high road and opted out of any further involvement. Soon, I would be rid of that area of the country, things were getting a little too real, even for me.

As I recite these tales of stupidity, I must point out, that there were MANY more times when I used a gun as a youth in a safe and proper manner. As a matter of fact, 98% percent of the time when using a gun, I used it in a completely safe and sane manner. Those events just have no voice here as proper use of firearms is expected and not really worthy of page space.

I would though, like to mention a couple instances that are actually heart-warming memories that perhaps could be placed here as somewhat of a mild balance. Memories such as a time when family members and I went out on a successful early morning hunting expedition for the next days Thanksgiving dinner, bagging a turkey and a couple rabbits for the table.

Walking through the woods during Christmas season with my girlfriend, scouting mistletoe up high to shoot from the tree with a shotgun. Skeet and reaction trials weekends where only clay pigeons, paper targets and eardrums are offended.

I would never claim that all the positives outshine the negatives though. That's just not the case with guns. People often die when mistakes and bad decisions are made with guns. I might also add that all children, if left to their own devices, will try on as many personas as present themselves. I did many things with a gun I shouldn't have as a youth and by saving grace none of my friends or myself were ever hurt. Luckily for myself and all those around me, none of these personas fit so I gradually and sometimes even abruptly moved on without looking back. I now also realize that with a bit more attention from my parents, I would not have done half of what I actually did.

At nineteen, I moved from South Georgia to Tampa, Florida. My first pistol was bought there. It was a Ruger Mark V .22 caliber target gun I bought with my first credit card at Woolworths. My second came soon after and was a 9mm, Italian made, P38 copy that I bought for $75 from the tenant that lived in the apartment below me. He was a Petty Officer in the Coast Guard with a job as a .50 caliber machine gunner on a drug busting Coast Guard Cutter out of Tampa Bay.

Enamored with guns, he owned many, and even had worn out .50 caliber bandoliers from his boat draped across the walls of his apartment as decoration. The 9mm pistol I bought from him also came with an under-arm harness holster, and on a couple occasions, I wore it under a jacket as "protection," when in dangerous places doing dangerous things.

Eventually, at twenty-one, I got tired of my life's situation and was ready for another change. Adolescent fun was giving way to adult need. At this point I had several different types of guns of many calibers and styles but their attraction was waning.

With very little hesitation, I sold all my guns for a handful of cash and joined the United States Navy.

In the Navy I was properly trained on several types of pistols and high-powered rifles of semi-automatic and automatic fashion, as well as different types of Missiles, Torpedoes and Explosives. I'll tell you, an M16/AR15 "assault rifle," is one thing, but an old automatic M-14 is my favorite "scary" rifle. Being abusively heavy and unbalanced, the slice-O-matic fore stock made gripping the bucking battering ram in certain prone positions a maniacal dance with pain. It seems strange in today's age that this gun was the high art of killing less than a hundred years ago. I became proficient with many types and many kinds of firearms as well as how to use them in unconventional ways, but the best training I ever received as far as firearms are concerned was thought training on how to think about using a gun and the consequences of pulling a trigger. Also very useful was how to defend *against* a gun in a myriad of scenarios. Much later in life it was this defensive training that ended up saving my life, not a gun. The kind of training that took into account an aggressor's *lack* of firearms training.

No longer having a personal weapon, while in the Navy I bought just one gun. It was a very small .32 caliber Derringer type to use as a pocket gun for defense.

Only semi-accurate to about fifteen feet, the kick of the round as it fired, actually affected the trajectory of the bullet since the barrel was so short. Yet, with my training, I consider this as perhaps the world's most dangerous gun. It was a large enough caliber to put a significant hole in a person and a small enough piece of metal to be concealed while still in your hand. I mean completely concealed in your hand, as-in nearly invisible, making it *very* dangerous.

It could be carried in a shirt pocket or even in a special pocket I sewed in the inside wrist cuff of a couple of my jackets.

(Idea courtesy of the "Wild, Wild West" TV show in the 1960's. I was definitely influenced by that TV show. I still hover on the re-runs when I find them today.)

The little Derringer pop-gun went everywhere with me and it ended up a stumbling block for my second marriage.

I still had this gun several years later after I was out of the Navy. I was in my late-thirties living in Seattle when one night there was a banging on the front door.

It was very early in the morning, around two.

I had recently been paying attention to a series of stories on the local news in Seattle where they were covering a string of home invasions in the area. This popped into my mind as I heard the banging on the door, so I found the Derringer before seeing who it was. It turned out to be a drunken friend of one of my kids. I shoo'd him away then sat down on the couch for a few minutes and consequently fell asleep. In the morning I woke in the same place and forgot about the gun that had slipped between the cushions un-noticed. Really, it seemed like what happened in the middle of the night before could have been a dream. As the law of Murphy suggests, while fluffing the couch, my Mother in-law found the gun right away. Both her and my wife, for some unvoiced reason, didn't believe the explanation when I recapped the strange events of the night before. I couldn't figure out why they thought that way and took the attitude that I was righteous. I still think I was righteous in action but I've long realized, not so in diligence. Since then, I've actually proven my actions of trying to protect from home invasion were justified. This little warble in time now seems as though it may have been a premonition of future events.

But again, I've jumped ahead a bit...

That was with my second wife, she was a naturalized immigrant from the former Soviet Bloc and had very little experience with firearms. She did not appreciate guns but was ok with them being around as long as she didn't see them.

My first wife's family on the other hand were, and currently are, enamored with all types of guns. Her father had many guns and cabinets for them all, all semi-safe and "locked" away. He gave my son a .22 magnum hunting rifle as a gift for his twelfth birthday, and later, I showed him how to properly use and maintain it.

My first wife's father had seven children, and all four of his boys borrowed their dad's guns regularly throughout their lives to hunt and screw off with. They seldom returned them in time and had no respect for guns at all as far as I could tell.

Any time I ever saw any of them with a gun, they were beaming with the attention they got because they were in company with that particular weapon. In my mind, they used guns to bolster their complete lack of self-esteem. None of them had permanent jobs, they were all on the take, and each had an addiction problem. Disgustingly enough, when her father died, all the guns were spirited away, before and even during, his funeral. That's how important guns were to them, screw the funeral, get the guns. Her Father was a very good man and didn't deserve that blatant disrespect.

One day while visiting at one of my wife's sisters house, my brother-in-law brought up the subject and produced an old Belgian .32L caliber Piper Bayard revolver of WW1 vintage. He needed money and offered to sell it to me. I wasn't so interested in the gun but I wanted to help him out, so I bought it from him and put it away for a couple years never using it. This pistol had originally been issued to an English biplane pilot flying for the French Airforce during WWI. The holster was stamped with an officer's name and claimed ownership of the 17th French Airborne, what great historical information. After researching the pistol, this became very interesting to me. This exact model gun under these same WW1 biplane circumstances, is rumored to be the kind used to kill the "Red Baron" in mid-air as a limping home Sopwith Camel Ace barrel rolled over him and shot him with it. Just being a piece of history, this gun turned out to be very interesting when imagining its previous life.

It came with three old, corroded cartridges. Vintage and harder to find, the only ammunition available for this old gun nowadays is the early lead ball type without a jacket so the gun couldn't be fired in an indoor gun range for target practice. This was a vintage pistol and came into the country as a spoil of war. The serial number had never been written down or entered in a computer anywhere for any reason. Never registered in any way, this is exactly the type and caliber of gun used primarily by the "Mafia" in the old days as a disposable gun for killing people. These old revolvers had only one safety feature, pull the trigger or don't pull the trigger.

I might add that I had children and my second wife had children, we were all in the same house together, but none of the guns I owned were ever locked away or themselves locked in any way. Similar, I might mention, in the same fashion to how I was raised. On a couple occasions I found them in a different state than when I left them last and was sure they had been played with. I chalked this up to the same ideals I lived by when I was young. After all, no one was dead, right? I merely found another "hiding" place.

This practice of barely hiding the guns had even bit me once before and I didn't take heed.

I was on something like my third self-applied slap in the face, when for reasons overshadowed, my first wife and I were in another argument. After a spell of yelling at each other from a distance, she appeared around a corner with her purse on her shoulder but seemingly had no plans to leave the house. With a little advanced maneuvering I got to the bedroom alone and discovered the Derringer missing from its place under clothes on the closet shelf.

To this I instigated yet another round of fuss, and on some unremembered premise we both exited out the front door of the house.

I then did a double take and walked right back into the foyer closing the front door behind me, quickly locking her outside with the gun.

[FOCAL POINT:
My children and myself were in actual danger at this point in time, she was in a very manic state. There was a scene, the police were called, she was found with the gun...]

I will concede to the fact, that in many relationships over the ages, men that have experienced extended hardship with women will at some point play the, "That Woman Is Crazy" card. Unfortunately for everyone involved, my first ex-wife had, and currently has, official paperwork with stamps in big red letters. She has been deemed mentally unstable by four States and the U.S. Navy. Committed to mental hospitals, put in jail and children taken away from her, she is a qualified mess. But if she wanted, she could easily buy a gun. Luck is with us all that she could never scrape up enough cash. Nuf-said.

I spent nearly a ten-year span with no personal guns. In those years, my time was spent making money, business connections and advancing myself materially. In the circles I was involved in, there was no need, or even talk of guns. Many of these people I knew considered guns a device of the lower classes, a danger to them only because one of them might get robbed with one. If any of them had a gun at all, their type of gun was a gold-plated presentation piece in a permanent display case hanging on the wall. Still, I would occasionally go to the local gun range and blow off steam. I'd rent a gun at the range from a selection of dozens. In these years this is where I took my children to teach them about guns. I got the impression that it was exciting for them, but none showed a rooted interest. The particular gun range I used was also a great place to teach them about firearms since that particular range on Seattle's East side is infamous for both the accidental *and* suicide deaths that have occurred there, three last I heard. I can think of no better place to teach gun safety and discuss misuse.

Overall, I lived just fine without needing a gun of my own for any reason at all. When I retired from the daily grind I had no guns. The .32 Derringer and .32L revolver had been given to my youngest son years before, and he still had the .22 magnum rifle his grandfather had given him also.

I am confident in his ability to use a gun and make competent decisions concerning guns since I am the one that taught him and have observed the results.

As far as I know he has never used a firearm improperly... yes, as far as I know.

Soon after retiring, I bought an RV, and my son and I did some traveling. We spent quite a bit of time in the far reaches of what's left of the wilds in the United States. We pulled a small fifth wheel trailer all over the country and beyond. We both agree that some of the best times we had were in the Sierra Mountains, Rocky Mountains and Desert areas. These places are also still full of Lions, Bears and other large and dangerous bugaboos of the wild, so we thought it prudent to have a larger caliber firearm. I narrowed the choices down by stopping power and cost then gave my son a pick from three models. His final choice was the Marlin 1895G, lever-action, .45-70 rifle. This is one of the most powerful of all readily available guns you can buy. This rifle can easily destroy anything it is used against, and a real pain to shoot since it literally kicks like a mule. A true eye opener, three shots is enough for a week till your shoulder bruises heal. There is also quite a range for types of ammunition. Everything from everyday "Cowboy" light loads to Elephant weight projectiles to Teflon coated armor piercing to honest to goodness spinning ninja type stars. We never had a reason to use it for protection, but did come upon the animals for which it was intended as protection. These animals made no intentions of us and neither us of them... luckily.

Besides, large predatory animals are protected by law in most wild areas of the United States and can only be killed if they attack, or by lottery when their numbers become a nuisance to humans. In our travels we did target shoot the devil out of our guns though. Both my son and myself enjoyed that part quite a bit, he's a very good shot with a good reaction time.

When we crossed the borders into Canada and Mexico, guns became a pain in the rear since if they even found a loose cartridge rolling around in your vehicle they could deny you access. Even though firearms are allowed to be owned under certain conditions in our largest neighboring countries, Canada and Mexico do not appreciate guns the way America does. We had to make arrangements to store all this stuff here in the States while we traveled there. True to my own past experience, we had nothing but fun and few worries in travel through both Canada and Mexico.

As we traveled outside the country, I did feel the absence of our guns and the security they imparted to me though. I have since thought back on this quite a bit. People were as nice as anyone could be, and even though on a couple occasions I felt uneasy, we never had a hint of needing a gun. As any good paranoid human would, I switched my security weapons to those available and had a knife at the ready for incidents of rabid raccoons and wandering drunkards. My feelings of such need for security aren't born in America though. A lot of people all over the world carry a knife for protection as daily practice. Also, my experience was not in the tourist areas. I found that the only place we ever really *needed* our weapons for protection was in the United States. There were a handful of scuffles in RV parks all over the country where several people had guns at the ready. Places out in the woods where people with crazy eyes held cocked guns as carefree as a lunch pail. People in such a hurry to get to the next stop light or highway exit, they flash you a pistol, to warn you exactly of who you are on the road with.

One day in November 2012 at the end of our rope while winding down from traveling the country, we stopped in a favorite RV Resort outside Hurricane, Utah. It's near the city of St. George at the Utah, Arizona, Nevada crux. My son and I were both ready for a rest during the Winter Holidays and were settling in to relax and spend time with family.

We decided that we were finished traveling this continent and had plans to volunteer for exploration of Asia in July 2013 as our next adventure on a five-month sign language teaching junket to the base of Mount Everest in Katmandu, Nepal.

Something I haven't mentioned yet, is that my son is Deaf. We had been traveling around the country and seeing the world for his benefit. I was trying to instill a world education as a self-appointed road scholar of sorts. I had already been all over the world in my life by virtue of my inborn wanderlust and years in the Navy and I wanted my boy to see how everyone else lives. These types of adventures are nearly impossible for most Deaf people and of course I want him to have the same chances for travel and exploration the rest of us in the United States have since the military is not an option for him as it is for many of us. The ability to travel the world unencumbered, to explore and learn is a great freedom. I feel, perhaps our greatest and most enlightening liberty as Americans.

So anyway... this last stop for rest in Utah was a definite turning point for myself and guns. As a matter of fact, it has been a definite turning point in thought for everyone I know, or even knows of me. My life is now defined as "before Utah," and "after Utah." A fact that itself is steeped in irony, being that my main life's focus has always been to try and define my life by the next thing that I'll do. Not to sit around in a vegetative state and re-live fond memories of my past. In my current life post-Utah, the best I can now do is to try and balance and meld the two distinctly different halves.

One afternoon, in the St. George RV Resort, (*it is now a KOA)* outside the town of Hurricane, alongside I-15 just south of Leeds, while sitting on the couch in my RV reading, the door was thrown open, and in jumped a man with a shotgun.
This man gave no warning of his intent, he didn't knock or call out. In-fact the only thing he said at all was to yell DIE DEVIL! He was in a methamphetamine induced trance as he shot me four times with the hunting gun.
The whole fiasco was over in the matter of fifteen seconds.

When hearing of this, people often ask;
"What? Shot four times with a shotgun and you lived?"
Yes, I "lived."

Of course, this needs a little more explaining. Nobody just jumps in anywhere and starts shooting for no reason do they? I must have called his mother a filthy lying whore, or at the very least, ran over his dog. I must have extended a lifelong torture on the souls of his family, a new found depth of the poon-ji mind screw he was intent on freeing himself and his loved ones from.

Well, let's see… it goes like this…

From the time we entered the RV Resort in early November 2012, it was evident this person was trouble. He accosted my son for cigarettes on several occasions in a drugged (methamphetamine) and manic fashion. He'd been a nuisance to everyone in the RV Park in this manner. Everyone there in the Park, including the employees, had a story to recite of how this person was a drugged-up nutcase. My son pointed him out to me on one occasion then told me how erratic and weird his behavior was. We agreed to try and avoid him at whatever cost till we left the Park. Not an easy task since he was in an RV spot just two spaces away, sitting in a lawn chair most of the day, chain smoking cigarettes outside his Fathers trailer.
We were there at the RV Park resort for the holidays being close to family in Las Vegas which was a short two-hour drive away.

This guy was visiting his father who lived as a permanent
resident in his RV, there in the Park.

A week or so after arriving, my son left for Seattle to visit his
Mother's side of the family for Thanksgiving and was to return
for Christmas to celebrate with my side of the family in Las
Vegas. I had just returned to the RV after visiting a day in Vegas
for Thanksgiving and this incident happened the day after.
Luckily, and thanks to advance planning and happenstance, my
son was gone for the holiday to Seattle.

...As I mentioned, I was relaxing in my RV, reading a book in the
early evening around 6pm or so when I heard a rustling outside
and then an overly hard and loud knocking on my door. When I
looked out the window, I saw this aforementioned person
standing there nervously fidgeting. When I opened the door,
there he stood, obviously drugged up and hyper. Grinding his
teeth and twitching, he asked if my son was there. When I told
him no, and why, his glazed look changed a bit. Without missing
a beat, he cocked his head sideways and demandingly asked me
for a cigarette. I told him; "*Sorry, I don't smoke*," and abruptly
shut the door. I'm sure I had a bitter, or at least a sour look on my
face when I turned away.

When the door shut, he immediately growled like an animal and
started shouting obscenities while smacking the side of my RV.
So hard, it was enough to make the whole RV shake a bit. He
stomped away cussing and yelled at nearby tenants as they
looked on. This was the end of my patience with this guy. I knew
that by smacking the side of my RV hard like that, he had
definitely left a big hand sized dent in the aluminum sheathing,
so I got on the phone and called the local sheriff.

Soon finished with my complaint, and assured they were on their
way, I sat down on the couch again with my book, but just sat
there intently listening to the goings on outside. I'm not an overly
aggressive type person and this guy hadn't been known (to me)
as an actual danger, so I didn't think of getting a gun out for

protection. He was not a big guy and not a very imposing presence. I was more beefy, and him being wiry or not, I had the feeling I could easily pick this guy up and toss him around if need be. I gave him no more weight in my mind than an obnoxious drunk teetering around the park. My son and I had seen plenty of those types in our travels.

There was a bit more noise and yelling going on outside as other tenants stared on, but it soon subsided and after a minute or so, I heard nothing more.

All of this happened in the span of five to ten minutes.

As I looked back to my book for a second, waiting for the authorities, I heard paced footsteps on the gravel in front of my RV. I thought it was probably the old guy parked next to me coming to talk about this guy, but within a second, the door of my RV was thrown open, and in he bounded. At this point he was no longer just some idiot drug freak causing problems. Since this incident, he has become intimately known to me. His name is Craig Manwill Bennett Jr. and he is a violent and mentally disturbed human being with a taste for methamphetamine. Check the post script in this book for an internet link leading to disturbingly short coverage of my incident with little mention of me, other than to say that the "victim," eventually lived.

He had gone back to his Fathers RV where he was staying, retrieved his Fathers readily available Mossberg 20-gauge shotgun, loaded it, then retraced his steps back to my RV. On his way back to my trailer, he traveled by foot carrying a shotgun, and even though several people saw what was happening, nobody yelled. Everyone ran without so much as a sound. All these people that sit around campfires with guns strapped to their sides postulating on scenarios of violence. All of these people that dreamed of being a "hero," with their guns spewing what they would do and how they would do it... they all *RAN* without a sound.

~ CHAPTER ONE ~

Apparently, a drug fiend carrying a shotgun back to the place he just made a scene at doesn't raise concern enough in modern America.

When I first saw him as he came through the doorway of my RV, it was the shotgun that caught my eye. I thought of the type and its capacity. I thought of where my closest gun was. My closest was that old .32L revolver I'd given my son, exactly behind me tucked away in its new snapped down holster. Easy to get, but first I would have to turn around and reach in.
My next thought was to turn around and get it, but there was no time, he leveled the shotgun at me and racked it within a half second.
Somehow, instinctively, I jumped towards him, first moving left then lunging to the right as he racked the gun. I skirted to the side and grabbed the shotgun by the end few inches of the barrel. As I had been taught many years earlier, this movement kept him from pulling the trigger as he tried to keep the long gun pointed at me. We struggled for a second, I had leapt ten feet and was leaning forward and off balance, he had a leverage advantage. The butt of the gun was wedged against him and a protruding wall and was immovable. In the struggle, within milliseconds, the open end of the shotgun barrel found its way to my left eye socket. As I quickly turned my head and pushed the barrel away, he pulled the trigger and a piece of the back of my head was blown away.

This blast threw me back and spun me around onto the couch to which he immediately racked the gun again and stepping forward, put the gun in my back and pulled the trigger again.
I was writhing as I felt the barrel touch my spine and moved just enough to where the blast went through the back of my right elbow, effectively severing my arm in two.
With my mind blurred, I struggled halfway to my feet again and heard him yell DIE DEVIL! as the shotgun's action racked again.

To this I somehow jumped out of the way and was able to yell, **WHAT ARE YOU DOING!** as the next blast ripped through the chair next to me, also shredding pieces of my clothing.

Again, I heard the gun rack and was able to consciously jump out of the way and onto the dinette table suffering little more than "pepper," to my legs.

As I heard the guns action rack once more, I remember thinking this was surely my end. I was thinking in packets of compressed experience that expanded into deep, meaningful and all-encompassing visions that I had been a part of. I remember thinking what a terrible end this was for my family and that I couldn't believe I was to die like this. I waited there for death, this was a five round gun and there should have been one shell left. I was now very weak and couldn't bring myself to move again. I laid there prone and broken, a sitting duck, I was fogging out.

A loud CLICK! was what temporarily broke that fog. Hearing the gun's firing pin fall on an empty chamber gave me a "second wind" of sorts as a mind-numbing yell in my head shouted,

..............*"JUMP FOR YOUR GUN !!"*

I struggled up as fast as I could and reached across to the void beside the couch where the pistol was. I reached with only the action of my right shoulder as I saw what remained of my right arm hanging limp in shreds, then without hesitation I quickly reached in for the gun with my left. Standing there with my back turned to him I yanked the holster snap off with my teeth. Spinning around I took a bead on his now wide-eyed head from ten feet away as he moved to jump out the door. I was able to pull the trigger and nearly hit him… I would have hit him easy… time for two… but intensely concentrating and spinning around I had become faint with these last desperate movements having run completely out of blood.

I was floating in a cloud as I turned to shoot and slumped to the floor in staccato slow motion, still able to see for a few minutes longer but now, completely unable to move.

In the next minutes, the sheriff finally arrived. A para-uniformed police officer appeared in reflection coming in the RV full bore, quickly asking blank questions... I heard muddled sounds and saw shadows of fading responders dance across the pools of blood I was lying in.

I could barely gurgle ....help...why?... why?...
Breaking free, I floated to the ceiling, I could see myself on the RV floor. I laid there covered in blood, akimbo, staring at the baseboard with a blank gaze. Then, to the tree outside my trailer, watching as my body was being lifted from the trailer onto a gurney. The offending shotgun was being held by an officer, it seemed bent and broken. Then again, my thoughts appeared in mid-air as I watched my gurney'd body being placed in the medevac helicopter on the highway, then...
...my Earth's consciousness was gone.

~

Many things have happened to my family and myself because of this incident. The effects have been personally devastating and far-reaching, but to tell you the truth... this book isn't about me. I recite my life's experience with guns to give myself credibility in the mind of anyone that reads this book. To let you know that I speak from where you are. I was you... I am you. Things like that don't happen to me and they don't happen to you... or our families... or our children.
That is of course unless your good friend and neighbor left their .38 special unlocked in the bed stand and your daughter was accidentally killed with it after school. Unless the meth addict that robbed your house, then used your gun he stole to rob the convenience store down the street and shot the clerk, leaving

him paralyzed. Until these things *actually do happen*, and no amount of imagination, speculation, preparation or paranoia will help you. None.

The TRUTH of these situations is, that guns for personal protection against guns is merely a security blanket for the mind. It is the rare instance when a gun actually thwarts a gun in personal aggressed circumstance. I applaud when that actually happens, but it is indeed rare. I applaud not because a gun's positive use gets validated, but because good has overcome evil…

…by whatever means.

The *facts* are, that there are more than Five Hundred, gun aggressed incidents in America for every one incident actually thwarted or stopped by a personal gun. In reality, when the decision is made to use a gun wrongly by an aggressor it's all or nothing and it happens *VERY* fast.

If you openly carry a gun in public for "protection," actual professional firearms training teaches you that you are doing nothing more than making yourself a target. It will be taken from you or you will be the first to die when the actual incident takes place.

This is basic weapons strategy training.

I speak from experience, but my experience is in no way typical. It is what you can expect in our gun bloated society but it's not what you'd expect from our country's free gun glorification. At the same time, it is just another blasé incident of a crazed individual with a gun. Nothing special in the eyes of the government or even the gun toting public. The incident of my shooting barely made the local news, had no follow-up and I wasn't interviewed by the press OR the police. Unfortunately, when people hear of incidents such as mine the most it does is to feed the American gun paranoia from both sides.

I personally know that it's the person at fault, not the gun, but that's always a hard idea to sell to others and here's why.

Something that comes to mind when people say, "It's the person not the tool," is that I can only wish that my attacker had a knife or baseball bat when he came into my RV. There is no question the results would have been at the very least, very different. But of course he wouldn't have come into my RV with a knife or a bat. By leaving the gun unlocked and available, his Father had given him a choice of weaponry and the shotgun gave him a sense of power that he was sure of. Even in his crazed state, his own self-preservation instincts would have kept him from trying what he did with a lesser tool.

So should I spend my time assigning blame?

Ok then, there are plenty of angles for blame.
He was on drugs, he was mentally unstable, his Father Craig Manwill Bennett, shouldn't have left a gun available knowing that his son was mentally ill. He shouldn't have been turned loose from jail after his last violent act.
If he was mentally unstable therefore not responsible for his actions, then who is? His Father? Maybe the RV park manager that knew of his issues and took no action to have him removed? Maybe the law enforcement and mental health systems that released him time and time again after committing MANY violent acts? I mean, dammit-all, he was released from jail from his last incident just a few short months previous to shooting me.

All of these are reasons for blame, yes, but none of these are real answers, none of them stick. Blame won't fix what has been done, nor will it stop any future issues. These are all just symptoms of what we have become as inattentive, blood thirsty, down trodden Americans. What are really to blame are the prevailing ideals and attitudes of the people within the United States. The clash of the pro-gun far right and the opposing no-gun, far left keep the rest of us in constant danger, blocking us from meaningful discussion.
We all stop at blame, feeling self-righteous in our personal views, then turn on the TV to see coverage of the next.

Even after all of this, even after exploring guns from as many angles as I can imagine and now living with the results, I am not against guns. I look around at the conditions of the United States today and I see a reality that unfortunately, requires guns.
I have owned guns, I have been around guns my entire life and there may be a gun close to me at this very moment. As you previously read, I had a gun just one foot behind me when I was attacked with a shotgun in November 2012, so I also get to call upon real world experience. What saved my life was not a gun. What saved my life was training. I didn't panic, I went for the gun, I didn't give-in and I lived.
If we are going to have such a gun-centric society, this is the type of training every single American should have.
Is that *really* something we want?

If you imagine yourself as some kind of badass with a gun, you should seek out actual professional training if you haven't already. A family member owning a gun, showing you how to pull the trigger and hit targets, is not training. The riddled tin can on the fencepost method is not firearms training. Actual firearms training is more than a three-hour carry permit course. It is more than motor skills and repetition. Actual professional firearms training includes how to think about guns in situations in which they may be used. How to think about taking someone's life and how to think about what you need to do to keep other people around you safe in the face of your gun and others.

If you have no competent training and own guns, if you leave your guns un-attended in any way, you aren't just part of the problem... *you are the problem.*

An irresponsible gun owner in the United States is a problem for the safety of our families and the people in our neighborhoods. These people are a problem for our town, our country and every person living in them.
And... I might also point out a little irony in this situation.

Un-thinking, un-trained and non-caring gun owners in America are also a big problem for the pro-gun movement.
These are the gun owners whose non-thinking and uncaring actions are eventually going to get America's guns taken away.

I admit, not a very good ending to our Love Story.

Put your sword away, imagination at bay
Let's live our lives as our own
Marching time is our foe,
Not the people we know
No weapon can help time has shown
Yet some will still fear those
Of conscious penned shy prose
As Dylan and Buddha and Franklin
Put down your sword then
No need of blind fear when
From out of its sheath draws... a mere pen.

Mac/

American Druthers

- Post Utah -

The first time I sat down and went over most of the ideas that now fill this book, was back in the Spring of 2013. The Sandy Hook school shooting from the previous December was still keeping the media busy, and my own thoughts on the subject were wrought with such indignation, I could barely stand myself. I had begun blathering for any and all reasons even closely related to the firearms issue, I was a wreck.
It was too much, *waaay too much.*
Unfortunately, it was what could be expected. After-all, I had been shot just two weeks previous to the Sandy Hook shootings and was so emotionally raw because of my own incident that I felt every death at that school, and every family member's angst as my own. Honestly, I still have a spell of outrage and flashback with every current incident that arises.

It's just not right.

For reasons not given much thought to at first, I sat on my couch at home during my recovery and started writing. I wrote and then when all else failed, dictated to people random. There is no real way to explain it, I felt like I needed to, I was distraught.
I now realize that my heart was broken. I had become manic as the desperation of my country sunk in. The country that promised me so much as a youth, the country I fought and killed for as a twenty something, the country that afforded me riches and baubles in my middle age, had failed me, and without hesitation, turned its back on me. And, I wasn't alone, it turned out as I dug in and researched that there were thousands of us. A sub-culture within another, within another.

A culture of friends, family and survivors of American gun violence that live their lives in an emotional limbo of unrequited love for a country that couldn't care less, as long as there is plenty of money on the table.

Since then, as I have met other people like myself and families of those now gone, I have begun to realize that we are all people of common background and thought. We are gun-culture shocked, pariahs to our people, all left hollow, all broken hearted.

From that bout I eventually self-published a small book that turned out to be what I now understand, is termed by the psychology industry, *a therapy book*. To explain what a therapy book is for those that aren't familiar with the terminology; writing a therapy book is a tool of action used in some circles of psychology to help those afflicted with post-traumatic stress, and other issues that weigh heavy on the mind.

Writing everything down from my own perspective and getting the poison thoughts out of my head without any outside judgment or baseless empathy, really helped to clear my thoughts and helped in getting me back to actual reality. A modern reality I found, that still couldn't care any less about my own personal situation. But after such deep thought and extensive research on the subject, I was able to better deal with the indifference I met. Bouts of PTSD still affect me from time-to-time and probably always will, it hasn't gone away. I still choke up when I think back to what happened to me. It always leads me down the path to thinking of the families I may have touched this way while contributing to their loved ones deaths during my Desert Storm military service. None of us realize the value of our human lives until we are confronted with the absolutes of death. I didn't know about the therapeutic abilities of writing everything down at the time, but felt so much better after getting to the last page and typing "The End." It felt as if a huge weight had been lifted from my soul.

All the angst and indignation I felt for my situation had been lifted from my shoulders and placed neatly in print between two glossy covers. Now, after this practice of thinking it through as completely as possible, writing it all down with no holds barred and then letting it go, I've come to more easily deal with the times when I hear of another shooting. I try not to listen to, or watch the news anymore, but that's hard to do. I keep a few copies of that old edition around my place so when I feel the need, I can rip one to shreds and throw it away... it helps.

That book was not really intended for sale, although quite a few were bought. Admittedly, that first volume was quite negative and blaming, not really suitable for public distribution. In general terms nobody cares about a subject if it doesn't affect them personally, and reading a book about some faceless angry guy and his sideways thoughts isn't on many people's to-do list. I can certainly understand, that type of read wouldn't be appealing to me either.

I imagine this whole situation I find myself in, *that we find ourselves in*, would have been a little easier on me personally if I weren't so invested on both sides of the issue. But lately, with the current attitudes of modern American life, it's been much harder to reconcile my neighbor's thoughts and actions with the highest level of living beings that we are.

But the world still turns...

As all things do, the wonder that never ceases finally does. What replaced that wonder is a measured sorrow and disdain in my mind for a culture that allows such things. These feelings have become the new floor on which my post trauma psyche stands. Then, what's left of life keeps moving forward. Leaving me, as all of us are, with life in the middle of perhaps the most non-caring, self-centered, money-grubbing culture on earth,
...with free-for-all guns.

Since that old therapy book of mine did its job, a lot has happened to the country we all live in. The thought patterns of our neighbors, and myself, have changed quite a bit.
Gun culture seems to have expanded on one end while people on the other end have become even more afraid and reclusive. People in the United States are more divided, paranoid and less willing to suffer the ideas of those around them. And I... I have become more thoughtful, more understanding and more loving in a reserved yet relentless way. Many see this change in me as becoming withdrawn and judgmental. I feel it as a discerning sadness. Most people that know me think that the piece of my head that was blown away must have been where my sanity was kept since I seem to be full of crazy thoughts now.
Do you want to hear one of those crazy thoughts?

Being shot, killed then brought back to the existence I now have, was the best thing that ever happened to me.

I can recommend it. Five Stars *****
Yes, that's what I said. *The best thing ever.*

Not so I can wag my finger, No...
Not so I can watch others go through similar circumstance as I, thereby validating my angst, No.
But because through my experience I have realized a part of humanity that we are all pulling away from, a part that we desperately need. Ironically, the specific part of humanity that drove our founding fathers to say "enough is enough," and create this great country of ours.
The part of us as humans that is fading in our memory is not paranoid delusions of grandeur standing on a foundation of entitlement, it is *intellectual morality*. The very founding principle of our country. The principle that says "All Men Are Created Equal," and that as humans with minds that think forward and backward, each of us have a moral standing of life, liberty and the pursuit of happiness.

These were progressive new ideas in the world back in the 1700's and we declared them on paper in the face of our oppressors.

Intellectual morality is a concept we are all familiar with. We generally don't think of it in those terms, either intellectual or moral, but we have all been taught or have heard the tenets of intellectual morality. Every religion on earth preaches this ideal in some way.

It is Benjamin Franklin's Golden Rule.
It is Jesus' instruction to his disciples.
It is a principal step of enlightenment for mankind.

Intellectual morality is the realization that all humans on earth no matter their sect, are equal and the same. America's founding documents say this is what we strive for. From the pre-amble to the last amendment of our Constitution, that is why America is here, as a shining bastion in the world for intellectual morality.

Many people feel, and I can certainly relate to those feelings, that in observing our modern-day American environment, many of our rights as Americans are being chipped away bit by bit, day by day. It seems that every little perceived offense of daily practice becomes a reason to either suppress or indulge a whine.
We are being forced to make concessions to engrained habits and traditions because others have no respect for, and perhaps feel no need for, the knowledge and abilities I, and others like myself, have come to cherish and see as our unwavering American rights. We have these rights afforded us by virtue of where we were born and where we live. More and more I see these rights being forsaken, adjusted and re-defined in favor of other peoples "needs."
Yet even though I sometimes feel this indignation and may get teed off, I am certainly not blind to the world around me. I know I'm not here in America alone, not in my town alone... not in my neighborhood alone.

Sad as it is, in America, in the twenty first century, we can't even be in the woods alone.

This itself is a modern circumstance that we will never be able to overcome, our population will continue to grow. More and more people in America, and less and less space to spread out into, pushes people together that might not have normally chosen to be together. We have a lot of situations in modern life similar to this that just simply weren't a concern in the early days of our country. Situations that don't fit into the definitions of previous need. Situations that we must reconcile with our ideals, our wants and our current needs, all the while considering that guns are in the mix.

To clearly think about this issue, we must pull away from the hyperbole that surrounds this situation and do some thinking for ourselves without corporate or political slant.

When our practice as Americans comes into question, we tend to get very emotional. Quite often we will grasp at straws trying to prove a point that we feel is correct but may have no actual basis. Something conspicuously missing from many important subjects in today's American culture of self, is in-depth thought. Thought that takes into consideration as many aspects of a subject as can be imagined. The kind of thought stirred up by those we still look to as our leaders. Great men such as George Washington and Martin Luther King. The men we revere as our American Founding Fathers such as Benjamin Franklin and Alexander Hamilton, men whose lives were defined by their train of thought. Truly, the most grandiose definition a human life can have is to be revered as a great thinker. Today we seldom call out the names of our great thinkers unless it serves our own purpose. These men (and women in some cases) thought deeply on subjects of humanity, taking into consideration as many angles of a subject as were presented in their day. Of course, they also knew that humans aren't perfect and certain topics of importance were overlooked or saved for later debate.

When these realizations came to light, they corrected themselves without selfish intent. Moving more towards the middle so that more people were able to realize the entitlements of being an American.

In America this is proven on velum as the Amendments to our United States Constitution, penned in part to release themselves from men of ill intent and limited thought. As Americans steeped in the history of great thinking men, it is abhorrent to consider that the one ability humans have, that no other animal on earth is blessed with, can be denied in favor of visceral emotion and the shallow want of material power. These being the very patterns of thought we opened new worlds to escape.

An idea of use being abused by its lack.

Then again, although all humans have the capacity for thought, it does not put us all on the same level.

"I think, therefore I am," is the basis for the highest order of consideration, not a basis of truth or ability, yet we can all learn. I am certainly no great thinker but I do think a lot and I ponder on a variety of topics. For instance, I think that the two most important attributes and byproducts of human thought are empathy and patience. I've thought about this quite a bit. Through empathetic thought we can understand our fellow humans and then if we must, through patience, endure them. We can see other people's point of view and adjust or wait them out. We know why others are happy and through this knowledge have hope for ourselves and those we love.

As humans tripping through our twenty first century, we have many topics of both past and current need, that beg for and deserve, a great deal of thought using patience and empathy. Some seemingly mundane subjects that surround our daily lives have been found to induce far-reaching reactions. A few of these urgent topics could use an in depth and thoughtful discussion.

Along these lines of daily mundane subjects with far reaching effects; I have also thought quite a bit on the science of igniting flammable solids, resulting in expanding waste gas. Are you familiar with this science? Specifically, how flammable powder once ignited, creates an expansion of waste gasses thus forcing objects from a confined space, say... through a tube.
I thought about this when I was young, and I thought about it in my formidable years. I thought about it as I transitioned to middle age and I've continued to think about this as I look back over the crest of the hill. As a matter of fact, this scientific reaction is never far from my thoughts. This kind of thought is a by-product of my culture. In today's American culture, all Americans are saddled with similar thoughts in some way.

It occurs to me now, in my "later" years, that up to this point, this particular subject of science has changed the world undeniably for the better. With the idea that "If a little is good, more must be better," we have now created an excess of this reaction, and like everything in excess, the potential of this particular science is now becoming a detriment to our society.
As I look back to how I thought of this subject previously and how I think of it now, I realize that by now, the end result is really what is truly important. How this science has affected us as humans over time since its inception may be interesting, but has little relevance when considering our future. How the current incarnations of this constant affect us right now, and where we see it going in the future is where we need to look. Not the action and reactions within our American history or how you and I personally feel on the subject. One truth of this scientific reaction that we've harnessed for destruction is; that without it providing a means, the world we live in would be a much more crowded place.
That's a fairly easy observation and won't get much criticism. Just think of all the people killed by expansion thrusted projectile since its inception.

We can easily say that over time, humans have used this science to severely stunt the population of the world. We really don't even need to get scientific or call to any currently groomed numbers. Simple math can give us a general idea. Think of the relatively small amount of people killed or maimed past further reproduction at Gettysburg during the American Civil War.

Let's use the nice round number of forty thousand. These were all men, and if they had Fathered children, we could assume each would have at least two. Some none and some eight, so let us fail to the conservative and say these men bore only two offspring, and each generation after did the same. Unlikely, but we will try and fail to the conservative.

If this were so, then in the nine generations since then, we have over 700 hundred thousand people eliminated from potentially walking the earth due to just one battle in the civil war. The number is actually much higher since generational time frames, moral age differences and longer life spans among other things aren't being considered.

Consider we started using this invention of mass destruction in this manner in the 1400's and just this year we will be rid of another couple hundred thousand or so. Being used to take these many lives throughout time makes this invention the world's most formidable tool for population control.

All aspects of humanity have been stunted in this fashion since the inception of this simple science.

Today in our hi-tech and infinitely diverse world environment we have destruction by expansion thrusted projectile down to a technological blastgasm. We can now destroy from thousands of miles away, we can destroy with a single pinpoint shot, or we can spray projectiles indiscriminately at the rate of hundreds of rounds per minute to wipe out any perceived threat.

One question that arises in relation to this ability is; what would we do to control our world and individual country populations if we were to rid ourselves of this favorite tool?

If we did that, then we'd have to depend on natural death, drug overdoses, car accidents, machete' wielding mass murderers and other death bent circumstance to keep our burgeoning numbers in check.

Unfortunately, to use any other tool at our disposal in the same fashion, such as let's say a knife or a baseball bat, our world's armies, street gangs and disgruntled employees would have to slash and bash indiscriminately and continuously for their entire natural lives to keep up. A human can only jab and crunch so fast and the intended victims aren't just standing there waiting to be done in, they run.

So, in the interest of population control and ultimate human power, we hold our lead thrusters dear...

How boring, have you noticed? I've been avoiding *the word*. How does that make you feel? Are you comfortable with it or does it irritate you? Were you getting tired of eight syllables in place of one? A fuzzy idea of the science of what exactly? Did you care at all? Did you think I was trying to use as many synonyms as possible to avoid using it?

Yes, in a roundabout way I was, all of this.

I did this to show how we can change the feel of a topic of conversation by just changing the words that we use. Next, notice that although the topic is the same, the feeling of this subject is about to change with the word I will use next.

What I'm talking about here under the poorly veiled pretense of expanding gas, is the "gun." A one-syllable catch-all type word that can evoke a feeling of security or a feeling of fear, a feeling of safety or a feeling of disgust. A word that has a different meaning and feeling for every person that hears it. The word "gun" is actually, a *VERY* powerful word.

People run when this word is yelled... and they should.

The word is as powerful, or even more so, than the object itself. But without all the blood spatter, wafting cordite and funeral arrangements.

A gun can be as simple as a spring action air rifle pitching a copper BB, or as hi-tech as a radar aimed Phalanx system spitting tungsten pellets at better than four thousand rounds per minute.

What a gun does for people, and the reason humans have such an affinity for them, is that a gun gives a single person or a battalion of people and even entire countries, the greatest amount of physical power a human can have on this earth.
The power to effortlessly kill and destroy is an awesome and absolute "godlike" power. This absolute power and the feeling that we as individuals can own and wield this potential power is intoxicating. Not intoxicating in an altered consciousness way of course, but in a visceral and primal fashion. An intoxicant that feeds the human ego and bolsters a sagging self-esteem.

If you were raised with guns all around you as most Americans in the past 240+ years have, you may have been raised with the idea that a gun gives you an advantage over those around you and the rest of the world. You can kill your own food and protect your family if needed. You can deter death and force others to your way of thinking. You can lead the righteous and thwart the invading hordes. All of this value can be had with the simple science of expanding waste gas in a tube.

Yet, I'd like to think that most Americans, be it of any political persuasion, if asked and given a choice, would answer that in a perfect world the American individual would have no need for a gun as personal protection or as an instrument of aggression. A gun would be thought of as just another piece of sporting goods for target shooting or hunting game.
Unfortunately, instead of a perfect world, we here in the good ole' U.S of A have a saturation of this science becoming a situation nearly the opposite. At this point in our country's evolution, we are killing ourselves at random and everyone within our borders is being threatened daily by a violent death. All for the abuse of in-depth thought.

I know that sounds a little off-putting, and maybe a bit extreme, but in the big picture of American Society, it is woefully true.

You read it in the first chapter, I am a deeply vested American, and also a victim of American Gun Violence. A born and raised United States Citizen at least five generations deep. Raised with "The Pledge of Allegiance," hand over heart with United States Navy War time service and because of all this, I know ***A LOT*** about guns.
In fact, I am in a club of people of which there are very few.
I stand with a clutch of folks that have a lifetime of training and use ending in an ultimate knowledge. I am pretty smug in the fact that in the whole world, there are *maybe* a few thousand others alive that have as much in-depth knowledge of firearms as I have. For people like us, our situation is pretty narrow.
That's a tall order indeed, and a claim that will bring more welcome criticism from those that have spent their lives in fear of, or obsessing over, guns.

But wait... don't get all bent out of shape as you think about who might know more about guns. Is it the model numbers, dates of production, size of your horde, ballistic specs or size of your manhood that makes you an expert on firearms?
No, of course not. Like everything else a person can have professional experience with, it is a rich mixture of the whole with a hard to obtain defining key that makes one a scholar of a subject. Something that not everyone can have and many don't want by virtue of the sacrifice it takes to get there. This defining factor is very hard to obtain and usually comes at a great personal cost. This is the very reason there are very few professionals and many competent drones. I'm sorry to be the one to break the news to those turning red right now, but owning a gun store or even being the head of the NRA does not make a person the oracle of firearms. What sets humans apart from each other is intellect, experience, and attention to detail, not their obsessive behaviors.

But really, all Americans no matter their history with guns, are on the same level when it comes to the mis-uses of guns.

All of this experience and knowledge gained over so many years by so many people on the subject of firearms and it all comes down to just one thing... *shoot or don't shoot.*
The human factor is what determines how a gun is used. No matter how many safeties a gun has designed into its mechanics, be it thumb, grip, half cock... whatever. The only safety that really counts is whether a trigger is being pulled or not, who is doing it and why.

I have observed more on this subject than most people, and consequently, with all my new found time, have thought and researched at depth on America's firearm attitudes.
After all of this extensive research, I've come to the conclusion that this entire subject comes down to this:

- An untrained person is unsafe with a gun
- A mentally ill person is unsafe with a gun
- A violent person is unsafe with a gun
- An immature person is unsafe with a gun

So how and why do these people get guns?

In the United States, the "how" is easy but fear is why.
Take away the fear and what is left is... we don't really know, we've always been fearful, we have never really felt secure, at least not in my lifetime.

Have we tried Love? No, judging from our past, and the current way we live our lives, we certainly haven't. Although sometimes love hurts, it will not kill you, I promise.
Sure, that sounds ridiculous, but it can't hurt to at least move in that general direction can it?

2019 total number of Gun Murders in America = 15,336
2019 total number of Gun Injuries in America = 29,646
2019 total number of Gun Suicides in America = 24,090

Total = 69,072

When was the last time you heard the number for gun injuries?

*Statistics are from GunViolenceArchive.org

American Druthers

- A Basis for Thought -

Here in this book I may sound a little stern at times. Truthfully, when it comes to this subject, I can get a bit warm. Before Utah I was of a right-minded persuasion. Although the reasoning is spotty, through my life experiences, I developed a deep-rooted respect for firearms and I imagined most folks around me, being gun owning Americans, were the same at some level. There were a few people I was wary of that had guns but I rarely worried about firearms at all, they were just another part of my life. After Utah, and with several years of firearms and social research under my belt, it almost feels like I may be the only one in America that isn't crazy about guns to the extreme. The right and left factions of our country have moved to either hate or love, with no middle ground. Both sides having an opposite reasoning, yet equal lack, of deep respect for guns.
I feel the left needs to respect the role that firearms have not only played in our past, but the role they play in our current lives concerning sport and protection. Conversely, I feel the right needs to develop a respect for the role firearms are playing in our random gun violence epidemic and the fear this instills in all Americans. I also feel that both of these situations can still be easily addressed with a little thought, and a lot of perseverance.

Of course, it's not just Americans in the world that seek out and use guns, that is certainly true. But many of the reasons that we seek out and use guns are unique to Americans, and that we have a free gun-for-all culture is one of several underlying reasons that people in other countries, and the governments of those countries, think of us, and react to us, as they do.

There are only twenty-four (out of 193) countries in the world where you can legally own a gun, and among those countries, we hold the per-capita "murder with a gun" record by far. We have more guns than people, and the loosest laws concerning firearms in the world. These other 23 countries also have guns, but Americans actually use them. The next country closest statistically is Yemen. They have 53 guns per 100 people to our 120 per hundred people, and most of Yemen's guns come from American manufacturers. Conversely, our death rate by gun is nearly forty thousand people killed each year and rising. In self-inflicted death, Yemen doesn't even make the top 12 list. Paltry per-capita numbers compared to The United States.
Yeah, we win. *

Just as seeing a person walking through the mall with a gun on their belt gives most people in the shopping center an uncomfortable itch when they notice, so is America's gun culture an affront to all other nations on earth, and they respond to us accordingly. Maybe not overtly, but it is a basis from which they begin all interactions. We are the escalators.
We are the self-righteous, self-entitled, self-killing, non-thinking, non-caring humans. The Americans.

That sounds a bit rough doesn't it? I agree, it does sound quite negative, but unfortunately it is also true. In my previous life travels, I've interacted with people in Europe, in Eastern bloc countries, South Pacific Islands, Canada, etc. and invariably I will be asked what I think of some American policy that they are aware of or that touches them in some way. Through these interactions the human aspect always overcomes the political as they realize I have no idea or control over my country's policies, and that I have similar thoughts as them concerning these political interactions. On a few occasions I have been asked if I had my own guns at home. When I've answered yes, a big smile and encouragement to tell them more is what happens most of the time.

Strangely, "Bang-Bang, Stick 'Em Up!!" is something I've heard more than once. I have also been scowled at, and lightly admonished for my country's policies and my own ownership of guns. Many outsiders imagine that we all wear cowboy hats and challenge each other daily in the streets. On the firearms topic, our neighbors to the north look down on us with contempt. I have had several Canadian friends and the thing that seems to stick in their craw the most, is our gun culture. When they visit the States, the Canadians I've known don't feel safe. When we Americans go to a city in Canada such as Vancouver or Montreal, do we notice that there are no guns around? These are large metropolitan centers that look and function just like our own, but gun violence is relatively non-existent. We are thought of as heathenish by much of the rest of the world. Starting with how we knuckle other countries under to get our way and ending with personal firearms. When looked at from that angle, I can see their point of view. From the outside, Americas attitude on guns and death seems as inhumane as any other claim of mass killings throughout the world. Our inhumanity as self-shooting, self-killing automatons has merely become normal within our way of life. Worse yet, over time, our guns have become protected by, and nearly synonymous with, American Capitalism.

Let's reverse positions here. Let us imagine that we, The United States, have just learned that Lower Slobovia was allowing their people to shoot and kill each other at random to the tune of nearly seventy thousand people a year. Upper Slobovia and the surrounding countries have been complaining about them for years. Would our American government have anything to say about that? Would the International community be aghast? If Lower Slobovia were a committed trade partner yes, we would sanction their economy and knuckle them under to get them to stop the madness. We would claim our moral superiority as leaders of the free world. The International community would be up in arms and create committees and perhaps even NATO would be called in with tribunals to uncover the depths.

Ok, back to our normal position...
Our moral superiority and hair trigger leaders keep the rest of the world at bay on the humanitarian front. These "lesser" countries will overlook our skeletons if they want to continue to buy our goods and to keep selling us theirs. This level of back and forth puts luxury and convenience on an equal standing with humanity.
Some will think this is a useless view. That this is what makes us leaders and winners. The ability to do what we want without accountability. I say that we are talking about our families and friends here, we are the ones dying. As a country, when we example this behavior, even on an international scale, it comes back to us as more of the same. It examples to the rest of the world how much we really care about humanity. With our entitlement, hypocrisy permeates. We are exampling that it is ok to some, and that we are no better, to others.

But how to change this? It has become the norm. The psychology of gun use in the United States is convoluted and engrained. After-all, they are easily available and nearly anyone can have one. They are easy to use and can be used again and again. People are afraid of them, yet are indifferent to the results. They are our largest threat readily-available, a knife, bat or car doesn't come close. They are impersonal in use, no need to look anyone in the eye. Quick, pick it up, shoot, dead. Even from a towering Hotel into the crowd below... and our founding documents say it's ok.
At least that is at the core, or default, of most arguments given.

"The Second Amendment says its ok. If some have to die as consequence to maintain my right to hold a gun, so be it."

That is not a direct quote from anyone in particular, just the default idea being presented by the majority of gun owners. An inane excuse for bad behavior.

I am sure for myself that the perception behind this idea isn't true, but I don't think gun owners realize this is how they are being seen by the left side of our own society as well as most of the rest of the world. This perception can easily be changed and makes me think of an interesting topic within the field of psychology, specifically, behavioral science.

Not too long ago I read a social study exploring reasonings for how people think and why they think that way. This study may not have been originally presented from the angle of how it is related to our firearms discussion but I think I can match these two up at a level a lot of folks can understand since we see this effect happening on a regular basis within our daily interactions with other people. I'm sure you will see a few similarities, I did.

First, *the words "ignorant" and "ignorance," mean that a person has no idea of a subject, or a limited view in comparison to the entire subject. They do not mean stupid in any way, ignorance is situational. The smartest person on Earth is likely ignorant on many subjects they have had little or no experience with.*

The Decision Lab is a think tank focused on creating positive impact in the public and private sectors by applying behavioral science. The following is a direct quote from The Decision Lab in reference to the results of the 1999 study named the Dunning-Krueger Effect.

"A common reading of it is that those people who are least competent at a task often incorrectly rate themselves as high performers because they are too ignorant to know otherwise."

Another might be, that smarter and more highly skilled people assume everyone can do the same and that the unskilled are so incompetent they can't realize their own ignorance.

Effectively: A person doesn't know what they don't know.

This idea is not new and has been stated by several people in several ways throughout history...

- *"A little Knowledge is a dangerous thing"* – Alexander Pope
- *"Ignorance more frequently begets confidence than does knowledge"* – Charles Darwin
- *"The fool doth think he is wise, but the wise man knows himself to be a fool"* – William Shakespeare

So, in our discussion here about guns I relate this social behavior effect as follows:

1) Firearms advocates see themselves as deserving and competent with guns. The Second Amendment states we are all entitled, and *most* advocates believe that any American can easily use a gun effectively/competently with no reason to be afraid since they see themselves as such.

   The reality of this situation is quite different with proof of this difference all around us.
   Purposeful shootings and murders. Accidental shootings. Suicide by gun and people using guns as threat for the smallest of personal offense happen by the minute all over our Country. This creates a deep-rooted fear of firearms, ability and entitlement be damned.

2) Firearms deniers see themselves as constantly in danger stating the proof all around us. They are generally afraid of guns and those that use them. Many claim the Second Amendment is no longer valid. They figure the obvious proof should be enough and that the gun advocates must all be uneducated and self-serving. Seemingly below themselves in a compassionately thoughtful and empathetic sense of the daily gun related tragedies that have befallen our Country.

   The reality of this situation is also quite different *with an advocates education having little relevance other than firearm training, and not so much as having a self-serving attitude as an entitled one. These daily gun related instances are happening to them and their families also.*

The truth of both sides, is that none of us know what we don't know, and we assume the rest from our own point of view, which may or may not have an actual basis in fact, depending on our personal bias. The problem with these two points of view is that both sides have friends and loved ones being killed and maimed. These points of view place us in a gridlock of dead bodies.

Today, as I write this, the proof is in the news. Three killed in California, nine killed in Ohio, twenty-two killed in Texas. All within four days. And that is just the mass murders. It doesn't include the nine individual gun murders over the weekend in Chicago or the literally dozens of other "lesser" gun incidents throughout the country that happened just yesterday. We pretend shootings don't even happen if nobody was killed but shootings are the majority of gun violence incidents in the U.S. Aren't we tired of waiting for the next? At this point there will always be a next. Two hundred fifty-three instances of mass shootings so far this year as of August 5, 2019. That number doesn't even include the literally thousands of "lesser" killings and maimings we hear nothing about. I was one of those...

I encourage everyone reading this book to go further than what is presented here. Seek out and try to understand new, different and opposing ideas. There are many angles and ideas in this book that can be investigated further and in much more detail, the internet is perfect for this. Thought is what makes us human, the kings of Earth. But the lack of thought and accepting the easiest way, or simply accepting what is given us because it satisfies our want is... considerably less than.

But, I feel my ire rising...
I just mentioned recent, senseless, mass gun deaths. I feel like I'm on the up-swing to a rant... give me a sec....
Ok, let's talk Peace and Love. There is a religious angle to be heard and this would be a good time to bring it up. We should also look at this issue from the angle of religion.

I would like to understand... I don't want to sound sarcastic but please tell me it is part of Gods plan. Then, can you adequately explain to me how and why?... and further, how could you possibly know? Faith? I'm sorry, but my faith was blasted from my head in 2012. I'm going to need something as cold and hard as the steel that shot me. And by-the-way, if God wanted me gone from Earth, he didn't do a very good job.
Or maybe he did a great job and this book is *your* wake-up call.

But... I'm pretty sure *Jesus* simply isn't excuse enough for the mother of a dead child. God provides no solace in the face of such emotional devastation. This kind of thing turns people away from religion rather than toward. A child that has yet to be fully tainted by life, shot dead. Isn't the purity of a child a sacred thing? Why would God will that? Can we get a reason other than "it's God's will?" I personally can't accept that reason. Isn't God on *everyone's* side? That's the same as saying that my family and myself are on God's (s)hit list. That's what it tells everyone, and those that are never touched must be the chosen... Except the "righteous," are dying alongside the heathen.
I say all this with a wry smile not out of sarcasm, but because it is so ridiculous. I am well versed in most versions of American Christian religion and I can tell you with certainty that there is no religious angle to be exampled here other than;
"THOU SHALT NOT KILL." As far as I have been taught, that wasn't a recommendation. There are no asterisks in our religious texts leading to a redeeming passage allowing killing if *WE think* it's ok. But of-course many scholars take other passages in the same religious texts as personal vindication of these heinous actions, somehow making it righteous, at least in *their* minds to kill in the name of their deity. Making, "In God We Trust," merely something to fill space on our money, and maybe a license plate.
From my experience, here's how I understand it;
If anything, *if anything at all*, God gives us a chance to prove ourselves as individuals immersed and faithful in his word.

But... victims be damned, guns feed not only our individual human egos but our collective American ego as well. We don't really believe in God, we believe in "me." What we are believing is that God hasn't chosen "me" to be killed yet, so I and my thoughts must be righteous.

Proving of course that we believe guns are greater than God. That's right, we don't know, we don't think, we don't care. Religion is an inane reasoning and provides no peace of mind when a church full of people praising his name are gunned down in the pews. Are *you* going to judge that they must not have been righteous enough? The reaper doesn't work for God by-the-way. It takes us all, kicking, screaming and scratching... ready, willing, or not. This is about us, we are afraid to die and we will kill anyone that we perceive is a threat, and that bar is very low.

"God damn you, I will come up with any reason that will get you out of my face, kill them all and let God sort it out."

...Is what I hear when God is brought into this discussion. This is how we relate to God and guns. Like God is somehow at *our* disposal. I recommend for our own religious good that we not invoke the name of God when excusing human death for reason of human want and fear. How ridiculous. Doesn't God know we have entitlement from a piece of paper?

Come on God, we even wrote your name on it in a couple places. We can't include God in this discussion anymore. He still lets us kill each other.

Being religious, and loving, and righteous in scripture is not a bullet proof vest. God doesn't judge us, we judge ourselves by our actions. The door to "heaven" merely opens... or it doesn't. The key to this door is our thoughts and how we have lived our lives. That's why it is so sad when people are killed before their time. We have a human lifetime to try and get it right... as long as we aren't sent to the "door," early, un-prepared.

That's why, *THOU SHALT NOT KILL.*

If we are religious, we know that killers take our opportunity for redemption from us. Whether we use that choice of redemption or not is our own divine choice. Killers take that choice from us. God gave us a mind to think our way around our troubles, not to create a means to kill our problems.
Is this all heresy? *I think not.*

Whew!... sorry. That's a sticking point with me.
Let us put the topic of God and our guns aside since we can't ask directly, other than to imagine what our divine entity might say or think based on books we ourselves are not wholly sure of.

Let's get back to real world why.
Why is it that some people in the United States have such an affinity for guns?
The short answer is MONEY creates POWER to induce FEAR. Then bolsters our EGO by suggesting ENTITLEMENT. That's the short version but these are all very broad topics.

Let's dip into each of these just a little bit to spur some thought by starting at the core of the situation, Money and Power.
By now, everyone in the United States knows that money controls everything, absolutely everything. Hence, those that control the money have the ultimate power. This subject comes up quite a bit within many different topics, and from many different angles. Many conspiracy theories start here, but here is where I will stop. This is no conspiracy, it's out in the open. No matter where it comes from or how it gets there, money makes things happen or keeps them from happening, this is a time-honored fact.

It has also been scientifically proven that repetition creates habit and in leu of a stronger need, changes thinking. Over time, the firearm industry, using its lobby in our Government, has used its money to maintain a repetition of thought and government control.

Many Americans, not understanding that they are being used in this way, become habitualized in the thought that guns are a safe, or at least ok, commodity to play with as anyone sees fit.

Americas firearms manufacturers have lobbyists, the firearms aftermarket companies have lobbyists, the NRA has lobbyists, all use as much money as they can to stop any hint of change that might threaten their profits. One might think this is un-American considering these entities bear a responsibility.

They are responsible for pushing as many guns into the public realm as they can with very little thought or action on consequence or personal human responsibility. They will tell you that it is the gun buying publics responsibility and take none for themselves. But they can see, as well as we, what their products are doing to our country. When you tie the hangman's knot and hand the rope to the distraught, you are complicit in their death when they hang themselves. If firearms companies want to be considered "people," as an entity, so they can contribute to this government control, they must also be considered people when considering the string of causation in American gun death.

As far as these companies are concerned, everyone in America needs a dozen guns of all shapes and sizes. They suggest all of this need, want and entitlement for no other reason than so they can collect the money.

NO OTHER REASON. They in no way care about your safety, they care about money. That's what business is about, money.

The Second Amendment is a built in, government guarantee that they will always have customers and that they will stay in business, them, and of course, mortuaries.

Now *THAT'S* a business model.

Sometimes I wonder if the general public knows what money is really for. Buying more stuff is just a pacifier that money provides. Money is actually an insulator, it separates us from others. Whether you realize it or not, that is why you want it. When you have no money, all you see is what you don't have.

But when you get money or already have it, shiny things lose their luster quickly. You will soon find that money can keep the boogey man away. The Boogey Man comes in many shapes and sizes. From living in a gated community to keep the Boogey Man out, to putting our children in an upscale school to keep the Boogey Man thoughts away. If we can make enough money, we don't have to worry about the Boogey Man anymore.

We can buy more guns to threaten and kill those that attempt... anything. Then, when we have ruined everything here, we can afford to go and live somewhere else. That's why the gun issue isn't as dire for the rich. Once a person has enough money, their attitude changes to that of a more worldly nature. We can heavily insulate ourselves from the realities of the little people with our money. If need be, we can pick a country we like and go live out our lives there. A country where guns aren't such a threat. Did you know that most countries have a number in dollars as to what their citizenship is worth? We can simply buy another life in another place after things get too crazy in America. What a great sense of security that must be. The lifelong hassle of amassing money does have its rewards.

Since a corporation is considered to be an actual person in our American Capitalist society, them having so much money is an impossible hurdle for the general public. After-all, it is our representatives they are buying off while we bleed. Their money works overtime in getting them just what they want (more money). While the death and destruction in our own country rages on. We can all see that the money they spend on our Senators and Congressmen has created a power that is hard if not impossible to get around. There is no avenue as such for the general public. Where's the Constitutional Amendment providing for public lobbyists?

Personally, I've come to think of it as convenient circumstance that Americans on the left are a more thoughtful and reserved type of people.

If the conservative far right were told to "suck it up buttercup," in this same way, all these guns we have across the country would no doubt be used to help change government thought. Without money and power from big business, Americans might actually be able to come to an amicable middle ground. This money drives us crazy.

Solution : *Take Away The Money.*

If there is no money to be had, or it is too expensive to maintain a profit, there is no reason for a company or "non-profit" entity to exist. The problem with this solution is that we aren't all on the same page in this book of the dead. It takes a concerted effort and solidarity of intent to shut down a sprawling capitalist entity. They insulate themselves with money also.

What about Fear?
Fear is the core reason we Americans have such an affinity for guns and it is money and power that supply this fear and keep the ball rolling. This is definitely so, yet very few people will admit they are controlled by fear in this respect.
You may ask; *Then why do they think they need a gun?*
And you will get many answers to this question, but the core truth to all of these answers is that people don't want to die, they are afraid of death. We are all afraid of death and afraid of the unknown. Protecting our things with the threat of a gun is a convenient benefit but we still can't *legally* kill someone for stealing anything from us unless they appear uninvited in our home or property.
We use the threat of gun violence in this way. We are told threat is one of the two primary uses for a gun but if we look around, we can see that isn't exactly working. Things are stolen daily from everywhere in the United States under threat of guns and it continues to happen at an alarming rate. There are more guns in America than people but this doesn't stop murderers, armed robbers and thieves from doing their worst.

Apparently, the threat of a gun isn't enough.
Proof enough of this to me is all around in my own environment.
Tucson, Arizona, where I currently reside. Tucson residents have
more guns in each home than I would like to imagine. Arizona
has some of the loosest gun laws in the country, yet thieves
regularly steal anything and everything that isn't bolted down.
The thieves don't care if you have a gun and they generally don't
have a gun themselves. They know that guns don't shoot
themselves and that people must sleep and leave their things unattended at times. These thieving people generally aren't killers,
they are thieves and opportunists. I'm sure that many people
reading this book know of an area in their town or county that is
rife with blatant theft, guns be damned. Some might say it's
because we can't kill anyone for theft and the thieves know it.
Then again, some might say that this blatant thievery exists
because of the separatist attitudes promulgated by money and
power. The same separatist attitudes used to keep us fearful of
each other so we will go buy another gun.

Fear is nothing more than self-induced mental enslavement, it
holds us back. Most fear is baseless, being situational and
experience oriented. We Americans live in fear someone will
take what is ours, fear someone will hurt or kill what is ours.
Fear someone will send us to judgment before we are ready. It is
a strange situation that more than half the country is not fearful
enough to own a gun yet the remaining are sure they are in
mortal danger at all times in their own home. Ironically, a lot of
this fear is because they themselves fear guns.

Then, there is Ego and Entitlement.
Americans have so much of these two that we have to carry them
around in a plus sized holster. These are our separate
psychological and ideological forces doing the bidding of money
and power. Our individual human lives are dictated by our ego *or*
lack of ego and our entitlement urges it on.

It is a grand sliding scale of humanity as to how much ego we have, but our egos can be increased or decreased by our successes and failures. Our self-esteem is closely tied to our ego and is a measure of how much we like ourselves. An interesting angle to explore is how capitalism is closely tied to these two human constants via the marketing of products and services.

Companies all over the world employ marketing specialist to devise sales campaigns to help spread the word of their products and to urge people to buy those products. These marketing specialists employ psychological tactics to either validate, offend or boost our egos and self-esteem in order to get us to pay attention and buy. One of these tactics is to appeal to our sense of entitlement. There are many sales tactics, including appealing to our sense of fear, love, libido, etc. In our case here, the firearms machine uses fear of other people, our love of other people, our low self-esteem and our Constitutional right, to sell us more guns.

"We must protect our loved ones from the blood thirsty invaders with our shiny and somewhat exclusive firearm because the Second Amendment says we can. We'll be heroes."

We don't just assume this small thinking works, it does work. The problem with all these sales techniques is that gun owners and non-gun owners are being killed at an equal rate and the guns they have been sold to "protect" themselves from this constant are not even making a dent in the situation. I've said it before and I'll probably say it again, less than one in five-hundred deadly circumstances are physically thwarted by a personal weapon. I'm not saying this is reason enough for everyone to get rid of their guns, I'm merely stating a fact of the situations we see in the news daily.

Speaking of facts, *what about facts and statistics?*

- Firearm Related Myths, Facts and Statistics

Especially on the subject of guns, people are wary of statistics gathered by anyone but themselves. Unfortunately, our individual lives are quite small, and the extent of our time and ability to gather the facts and statistics is not well honed. So much so, that we don't personally gather any statistics at all. Besides, there are campaigns on both sides of this issue to discredit the other sides so-called "facts."

Why bother when we can go to our favorite news outlet and get the numbers presented in a way to appease our mindset? Many won't trust the government to gather these numbers citing an all-encompassing agenda of control. Very few will listen to anyone on the other side of the issue and if facts turn out to be inconvenient to our cause, we tend to sweep them under the rug. There is a lot of ego and self-esteem to protect on both sides of the American firearms issue.

But this is all about thought, we need to expose ourselves to other people's thought unlike our own to see how and why others think and feel the way they do. *It does matter.*

For instance:
www.americangunfacts.com

This one-page and somewhat cheesy looking website sets forth disingenuous claims that are directly opposite of what has been represented by nearly all other sources. This site offers citations for its gun image tables and pro-stance claims, but if you actually follow a link to a citation you will find that they have used information sometimes as old as 25 years alongside information 10 years old from a different source and placed them in the same table, apparently claiming one validates the other.

There are no current figures on this page and many completely false claims. The person that made this page is not doing his pro-gun cause any favors. There isn't even any contact information, only a means to "Take Action," via Facebook and Twitter. In my mind, that means this hidden entity feels that they are beyond reproach and their disingenuous compilation of numbers should be enough. Apparently, it actually is enough for 3.2k Facebook "likers." *(Nov. 2019)* A number that proves the pages worth. Considering the amount of time this page has been up, that number is ridiculously low. By contrast, anyone could make a Facebook page to say that they wanted to marry a gun and it would get 10k likes in twenty minutes. It warms my heart a little, people aren't as oblivious as they sometimes seem. At least those that haven't followed the "Take Action," links.

Yet, the same type of thing can be said about the gathered tables set up by left wing news sources. Their information may be up-to-date but the placement and tone of their narrative alienates the people that they say they would like to sway. They are doing nothing more than preaching to their own choir of viewership. We also can't forget that most of these news sites offering us information and statistics on the firearms subject are entities that sell advertising, meaning that they pander to a narrow audience for their worth. These examples are the definition of "Fake News" on the internet. Narrow minded web page and blog owners, thrusting small shoe ideals and news for sale. Anyone can create a web page, and if you choose to believe what's there because it validates your personal feelings, you become part of the problem. Take in as many angles as you can, think about reasonings and agenda, then research some more. It is a tough business to find truth in todays divided American society. I would recommend searching out information from a site that has no personal agenda. A stand-alone entity with no advertising, no editorial and easily validated by *current* citations.

We can't just throw any numbers around and make claims so they fall where we want them. Other people are paying attention. If not to learn, then definitely to ridicule the ways and means used by the other side of the discussion.

Let's discuss a few myths and claims about guns and the people that use them from the standpoint of common sense. Perhaps shedding light on why they are myth or truth. Most myths are based in truth but skewed in presentation to benefit those offering the idea.

Sometimes wrong ideas are even presented on purpose for an intended benefit that we may not be aware of or even ok with. Truths presented wrongly are a detriment to any side of any discussion. People aren't really stupid.

Let's start with the big one...

Guns don't kill people, people kill people

This is so obviously true, it goes without saying. Everyone realizes this whether they acknowledge it or not. The problem with this statement is that it is used as a retort when all else fails or, a mantra to blindly repeat. Being obviously true doesn't negate the fact that less guns means less gun deaths. Which of course is the opposite side of the discussion and another obviously true retort. Neither is worth repeating again and again as a point. The point is taken.

The only thing that stops a bad guy with a gun, is a good guy with a gun

This is true to a point. To make this an absolutely true statement, we would need those "good guy," gun carrying Americans to actually use their weapon in the defense of other people, this is not happening. A gun does not make a person a hero. Most people that have a carry permit and actually carry their gun around with them do so for their own protection, they are "me" people. The truth is that most are scared, and sorry to say, somewhat cowardly, they carry for threat and ego. Most are also not confident in their abilities and knowledge of these violent situations and are wary of the consequences that may befall them as a result. In short, they aren't trained.

I mention again, painfully I'm sure, how less than one in five hundred firearm aggressed circumstance are thwarted by a "good guy with a gun." The opposite argument is that these positive stop circumstances aren't being reported.** But this is an apples vs. oranges comparison. I'm talking about stopping a shooter with bullets and they are talking about threatening before anything happens. I can believe that the number would go up to 5/100 if we include their end. Still nowhere good enough to use as reasoning. The proof is in the news daily. Guns don't change human nature they exacerbate it. You read a little earlier about my own personal experience with this situation.

"Stand Your Ground" laws are needed everywhere so citizens can defend themselves

There is no law that says you can't defend yourself. Americans can defend themselves by any means available, at all times, against any *credible threat*, no matter where they are in America. The issue with the stand your ground laws is that it sets a line that can easily be crossed without thought as to consequence. It makes it too easy to go too far. Shooting someone for pushing you down is not a reason for deadly force. Being threatened with a deadly weapon or honed physical ability *is* reason enough. If we are going to have laws like this, we also need to have training nation-wide on the definitions of deadly force *and* the threat of deadly force. These laws give a person looking for a reason, a reason.

We don't need new laws, we need to enforce the laws already on the books

Gun laws and restrictions don't work for a couple of reasons. The first being that guns don't kill people, people kill people.
The second being that there are fifty states in America and all of them have different and sometimes opposing gun laws. The only laws that will ultimately work are actual people restrictions concerning firearms and only on a Federal level.

Mass shooters specifically target gun free zones

This is an incomplete and somewhat sideways thought and shouldn't be a part of any discussion on firearms. A "Gun Free Zone" is only there to give those that use the space a small sense of security considering Americas gun situation. Any police or security officers in that area carry guns as they normally would. I seriously doubt that any shooter takes this into consideration. In case people haven't noticed, most mass shooters expect to die when they commit these acts, it's part of their plan to go down in a blaze of glory or death by cop. A gun free zone works against that plan. Besides, there are more people carrying a gun in their purse or under their jacket than we know. Out of sight, out of mind. No sign can tell if a person has a concealed weapon. A true gun free zone includes a choke point where a metal detector and searches are taking place.

The Government is coming for our guns

Slippery slope theory aside, which at the rate we are going would take a thousand years or more, there is no *real* evidence of this. There has been no serious legislation even offered up for review as to taking guns from people. The most we have going is the talk of assault rifle bans and similar guns that have no viable use in open society. That is not taking, that is removing from sale. All existing are still legal. Even if these guns and accessories are eventually banned, the ones already out in the public will be grandfathered in up to the last serial number made the day before the ban. No one will be going around collecting these guns. At the most, the government might offer to buy them back. There will be no requirement to turn them in. That would be taking guns, we can't do that. What's really happening here with this callout is that all of the fervor and talk of weapons, the attempts to ban certain guns and accessories and the far lefts continual push for eradication, evokes an atmosphere of the slippery slope theory come alive.

It *feels* like our guns are the target of destruction, but in the big picture, it's not really so. This idea is nothing more than a cry to incite radicals and circle the wagons during a discussion.
Sad truth? Our Government wants us to have plenty of guns. The firearm products stimulate the economy and the death... stimulates the economy. *(hopefully questionable)*

Violent video games, movies and events are to blame

Yes, these things do de-sensitize us to violence, yes, they do skew our morals and feed masochism. But from there to killing people is a big step unless a person is mentally ill to start with. I believe that killing other humans is not in our souls, Love is in our souls. We need a reason, good or bad to kill people. To emulate "entertainment," is not a reason that the human psyche will stand... unless that mind has been previously broken.

How about; how the political left uses the gross numbers of American death by gun as the number of total aggressed killings every year when 60% or better are actually suicides? The right claims this total number displayed as disingenuous, and they are correct. Of-course it's *all* death by gun.
How about; how we conveniently leave out the injured and maimed number when making these claims.
The word "Deaths" may have more bite, but it hurts the discussion to leave out the other 25+ thousand injured people. It is all gun violence.

So how and where have I found my information?

You have read a little about my life, which is where a lot of my knowledge comes from, but I've used statistics and history from several places. I have read many websites and gone down many avenues only to be disappointed by tone, intensity and hyperbole that shouldn't be there when delivering the facts. That is not Journalism, that is editorial and posturing.

If any "news" entity can't get that right as a starting point, they are nothing more than a pandering, fly-catching pile for our society. Worthless to all but their advertisers.

News outlets are for telling us what went on today. Statistics are not about what went on today, they are numbers compiled from historical fact.

We can't charge that an entity compiling statistics on gun use and deaths is making up the numbers simply because they are not of our political persuasion, although, they may only present numbers that benefit them. That isn't statistics. Statistics are hard factual numbers that take no sides. All statistics on any subject will be the same or similar, no matter where they came from or who compiled them. The differences will be in how they are presented, what is left out, what is added in... and why. Editorial slant is one thing, hard factual numbers are steadfast and real. If we don't like the numbers or statistics presented and somehow think they are wrong or skewed, it is up to us to prove that by gathering them ourselves. Not walk away and ignore the rest, which has become quite common.

I have trusted The Gun Violence Archive and the Gifford Law Group, among others, to gather and present correct numbers. Considering the horrific vetting Gabby Gifford and her family have already gone through, her being a conservative lawmaker from Arizona and also a gun violence victim. Ms. Gifford was a Republican Arizona Senator that was shot in Tucson, Arizona in 2011 along with twelve other people, six died. She has been shocked into reality, and along with her Astronaut husband Mark Kelly, have championed reforms that do not include taking guns away from people.

I've checked the citations on their site and tasted for tone, they have passed muster so-far. They are on the side of less American gun violence. It is important to understand where the money, power and ego are when researching anything of importance. These are the *real* enemies of truth and justice.

By-the-way, the majority of *my* ego was blasted from my head in 2012. I now hold only the power of the pen and my sometimes pushy, righteous indignation to oppress people with.

Also, if you weren't aware, this is a self-published book. Self-published books are by-and-large not big money makers. If this is a hard copy you are reading, you may have been given this book for free. I intend to give away as many as my monthly stipend will allow.

This is not about money to me, this is about my country. Self-published books are generally labors of love, hope, and because of their limited marketing, futility.

I write this book out of Love, and Hope for America.

To get Americans thinking. That is *my* only agenda.

As futile as it may be.

*Listed next are the external sources I have used for statistics and historical information throughout this book. Also, a couple great reads on the subject from unusual sources.

The Gifford Law Center - https://lawcenter.giffords.org/facts/gun-violence-statistics/

The Gun Violence Archive - https://www.gunviolencearchive.org

American Heritage - https://www.americanheritage.com/america-gun-culture

Guns and America - https://gunsandamerica.org

National Catholic Reporter -https://www.ncronline.org/news/opinion/faith-seeking -understanding/america-addicted-guns-and-were-denial

Pew Research Center - https://www.pewresearch.org/fact-tank/ 2018/ 12/27/facts-about-guns-in-united-states/

The Declaration of Independence, The Federalist Papers and The United States Constitution

** Verified defensive firearm use incidents are being documented on gunviolencearchive.com

How words make us think of actions that stink
As shoe tread now sullied with poo
Old sayings we scoff, as we flip them off
These words shouldn't hurt but they do
Sage phrase pass the test, of time guilt and jest
Too hidden, yet open to see
No argument will work to
Bring solace upon you
These words often painfully true

Mac/

American Druthers

- What Is It About Us ? -

A good practice for us humans to take part in, is to explore how we react to our environments and why. This has been a practice of the upper echelons of power and commerce since the beginning of civilization, this is how people are controlled. How do humans think, and why do they think that way? What do they like, hate and fear? What are their incentives? I partake in this practice of observation and introspection and I have found one thing that is absolutely sure;

Humans do not like change.

Can I say that without being heckled? It's not just Americans, oh no, every human on earth would like to stay right where they imagine their glory days to be. Not only is it fundamental to our very existence, it is also a basis of truth, being one of the few constants there are in our entire world. It is absolutely true... Everything Changes and *we-don't-like-it.* Everything from the start of wherever we agree to measure time from, has changed. It all started there and changed till where we find ourselves at this very moment. Change both good and bad has come but if you measure the big picture, as in fig leaves are bad and moisture wicking clothing is good, *(archaic vs. modern)* then good has won and seemingly always will.

Change is nearly always good, it stirs the pot and the mind. We humans want to stand still and enjoy the fruits of our past labors but change won't let that happen for very long. Change has spurred thought and advancement in human beings since the very beginning. Change is a bittersweet mistress.

When someone mentions that a change in something is always good, people often ask; *If change is always good then what exactly is good? Who decides what is good? Why is it good?*

Good is decided by the *changing* and ever evolving morals under which we live. Not long ago it was within our American collective morals to sentence someone to death by hanging, we thought that was good. We kept our women's ankles covered and denied humans unlike ourselves basic human rights, we thought that was good also.
There is no denying that change is inevitable.
The best we can hope for is to see change coming and try to get ahead of it. Or maybe to take part in molding the change to better fit our cause. Otherwise we can either conform to change, whine about it or temporarily obstruct it.
In the big picture, we cannot stop change.
Disliking change is a human nature, what is not human nature is to head a problem off at the pass. That requires forethought, which is seemingly a lost art in today's modern society. In general terms, we Americans only think far enough ahead to plan for our next vacation or large purchase. Getting ahead of an issue is certainly within human ability, but not nature. This is actually a valuable skill that must be learned. Once learned, life becomes much easier, but unfortunately, America is full of unskilled problem solvers... with red faces and ulcers.

Something we all like to do is to stand around whining and wait for someone else to do something. Not taking the initiative to solve the problem ourselves but to put it off until the last minutes or hope that someone else will take up our cause. This procrastination makes everything having to do with solving any problem much more difficult and usually much more expensive. So, humans stand around and wait some more. We may have a low self-esteem and are afraid to step out front in case someone might think bad of us in some way. Or this might cut into our money, change is expensive you know.

This low self-esteem problem America has, is now becoming a problem on a grand scale.

Our Corporations have enlisted psychological marketing campaigns to tear down our esteem so they can sell us the products to build it back up to where they say it ought to be. The problem is, when we get there to where they say our esteem should be, there is another reason waiting for us to feel not good enough. Many of us bombard ourselves with violence for profit so we can momentarily live in an environment where our imagination makes us strong. Sometimes we struggle to buy an item we can't afford to help fill this gap we feel ourselves in. We buy things so that we can fit in somewhere others think we don't belong. We tell poor people they are lazy, we tell the middle classes they need to buy, buy, buy until they drop or they are a failure. We notice that we never tell the wealthy people anything so let's all try to be wealthy, then our lives will be good. *Not true at all.*

All of this, and much much more, raising our stress levels to the roof. The percentage of winners in this materialistic shell game are measured in decimal points and then held up as hero's for others to once again follow... and the circle continues. It all leaves a very bad taste in the mouth of those with less education and in the lower levels of our society. A bit of in our face proof just slapped us pretty hard in 2016. Look how many Americans felt they needed to help "Make America Great Again." No matter how you feel about that, what was important? Things changed. We can all see what's going on but still we tend to stand there waiting for others to act, waiting for our ship to come in.

"That's what we have Government representatives for," is the most common answer when the frustration gets to be too much. Remember them? Those people we paid four minutes worth of attention to six months ago. The same people that are trying to enter the grift machine and get their bag of money the "easy" way. Then we spend a lot of energy whining about them.

The problem is, they are in on it and are working hard to perpetuate the situation. Sometimes we can't even get them out of office once they have the machine working for them. It's a very disconcerting situation and one that may be impossible to get away from without some sort of national awakening.

This isn't a book on the spider web economics Americans live their lives with, or its effects, other than to mention that this situation is real, and plays a contributing part in America's firearms attitude.

There are many types of people in America and each is focused on their own situation. As people try harder and harder without their conditions of life changing, or they find it's not plausible to become what they've dreamed, as a matter of course, disillusionment sets in and many find the only power they control has a trigger.

This power is cheap, this power is available, and this little piece of power is protected for all to have. No common, every day, bad life decision can call the repo man to take this ultimate power away. Paranoia then becomes the norm because there are a lot of people living in this condition, we have to protect ourselves from each other now. Soon everyone else that hasn't been beat down enough becomes the enemy. We end up with race on race violence, poor on poor theft, seething racism, gangs on the streets in place of patriotism, motivational speakers and then the worst of all, books like this one.

A common tool used against us in these schemes of control is the fact that we don't want to die, this is an imperative in our lives. Although all religions are based in preparing their people for the next life and are supposed to relieve this worry, to spite all that, fear of the unknown rules our lives. This fact falls neatly into many sales schemes to keep us in the circles of control I have previously mentioned.

Mortality also feeds sales of many items as well as raising stress levels and feeding paranoia.

It also creates a little circle of its own; afraid to be killed by violence we depend on a gun's implied violence to deter this perceived violence.

This train of thought randomly backfires and we end up with an otherwise decent person in jail for assault or murder, or worse, dead, as they insert themselves into situations based on the false security of their gun. We often find people wearing a gun cowering in a corner instead of stopping the violent take-down robbery with their weapon like they swore and bragged and imagined they would.

Mob mentality and following self-serving ideals are something to explore. These are common practices found among those of simpler intent. What seems to be hard for these people to understand by virtue of them actually being less observant, is that the stance of "No," and vehemence of "Yes," contributes to the gridlock of thought, and deaths of our loved ones. Some of these people get adamant to the point of physical violence. Having no self-control, and resorting to physical violence, of course being a vestige of the feeble minded. If not physical violence, then violent rage and blathering obstructionism.

No matter what concessions are offered or ideas are brought forth, people with extreme views seldom give in till they've blocked any progress. Imagine... being blocked by radical people that are not self-aware nor do they have the capacity to see a bigger picture without putting themselves in it.

Ugh, what could be worse? ... Oh yeah, *a dead child*.

These traits we see all around us are all part of human nature and are exacerbated when we are treated by our government as pawns on a golden chess board, we follow, we hope, we fail.

Even more...

Of-course nobody likes a selfish attitude. We may all have one ourselves on certain occasions, on certain subjects, but we can all notice selfish intent in others.

Partly because we have so much of our own, you know the old adage, "takes one to know one."

Entitlement is a condition where one takes on the idea that they deserve. It may in fact be true that they have worked for this situation and they are now deemed deserving therefore entitled. The word "deserve," implies a function of value before hand granting this condition, the word "entitled," does not. Entitled imparts that you are deserving by virtue of decree, in affect because someone else says so.

It is good to know these skews of language out in the open so we are all on the same page. We all need to be on the same page, because everyone knows that Americans are entitled to every little thing they have. We are selfish as a whole, and selfishness is really the root of all evil, money is merely a favorite tool of the selfish. Americans are entitled and selfish, and love money more than life. Everyone throughout the world knows this. We call out to it from every angle. We have long lists of entitlements and for many different reasons. It's one of the reasons we are scorned throughout the world as bullies. We do things because we say so. "Because we say so," is entitlement and we don't like it when other countries say this to us. Their point of view would be valid if it were our point of view. When countries give us this attitude, we become indignant, pointing to our way of life as so much "better" than theirs. We must be better, therefore entitled. We measure our entitlement by power and money but some countries measure it differently and consider us money grubbing heathens to be ignored.

Many other countries give more weight to society and religion than we do and because of that, they feel entitled, at the very least, to be left to their own devices without our intervention. After all, our American society is a hedonistic mess. We have our own problems with crime and poverty and corruption. Who are we to say our ways are better than anyone else's?

The American argument abroad is a reflection of the American arguments in our own society. Each person's inflated feelings of entitlement encroaching on the next persons creating more discontent, more gun purchases. We've even devised a way to creep into the world and affect others this way. This way we've created, feeds on itself in an ever increasing and enveloping fashion with no end to be seen.

Capitalism creates a teeming society of self-centered "me" people. Each worried less and less about anything that doesn't directly affect them personally, but always ready for a money-grubbing fight to protect those rights to which they've already been entitled. Easy to see from the outside looking in, very hard to reconcile its worth in the big picture and impossible to even imagine with pockets full of money.

What's at the root of this ? The actual reason for us all to not get along with each other? Not how it applies to you specifically but where does it come from?

Our human nature is being used against us, by our money-grubbing Corporations, and their Government henchmen.

We will never realize this answer as it applies to us, until we take ourselves out of it. The selfishness we have been entitled to actually clouds the truth. All problems have a root and addressing this core reason is the stumbling block we have to solving these problems. We address them as they apply to us personally and how they affect *us* and how *we* feel about it. Blah, blah, blah...

Have we forgotten about our Grandchildren, our legacy, our heritage... our responsibility?

Do we know why our staunch Constitutional Representatives blindly spew nonsense, why the far right is so vehemently opposed? Sure, it stems from money on one end and low self-esteem on the other with a finely managed blend of iniquity in the middle to keep the cause viable.

Maybe people feel inferior because they have the want but don't have a better reason. Maybe they feel threatened because they aren't really sure if they will be culled as undeserving. Maybe they don't want the rest of us to know that they aren't as pure as they seem to be, as pure as they have built themselves up to be. Their status took a lot of time and money to nurture, creating a sense of security in themselves that we may be threatening.

Helping to drive these feelings of inadequacy are the made to please "News," outlets our freedom affords.

It is within human nature to seek out, listen to and agree with ideas presented to us that closely match those we currently hold, we want to be validated. Even if those ideas we currently hold were insidiously placed in our heads by the same people we look to for this validation.

MSNBC and Fox News, among many others, being purposefully contrived devices for the disillusioned. The people that run these editorial networks are merely filling a void and raking in the cash. Situational opportunism is alive and well in our fringe "news," networks.

The personalities and segments are juggled purposefully to feed the ideas of the downtrodden that they have helped to instill and then add to these with more disingenuous hyperbole and indignation. *The sole intent is not to inform the public, but to sell advertising.* Once again, it is money being chased. Money paid, for advertising that caters to the crowd of home bodies that faithfully watch and want to believe any "news" presented. Through Fox and MSNBC news networks, *(again, among many others)* these people are vindicated of their own failures as they are told it's always someone else's fault that we are in the situation that we are in. These types of "news" outlets have to maintain this fervor of indignation at whatever cost to keep the ad revenue rolling in. Nothing against anyone there of course. They're just making money in the approved capitalist model. *"If you can... do, make money at all cost."*

There are no laws against open, carefully worded speculation presented as fact, whether it be completely wrong or half-truths. Either way, it helps to fill a void by presenting the idea that our failures are someone else's fault. In Fox's case, they pander to the far-right republicans. The people being taken political advantage of that will never realize the fruits of the ideals they've been sold. In its own way, another subversive plot to take our American entitlement of free thought.

Of course, to be fair, MSNBC, Salon, Mother-J and those types fill the same spot for the left wingers and their ideas of pacification. They are no different, but it is interesting to note, that MSNBC and the many other liberal news outlets aren't called out near as much for their erroneous tactics and stances. In fact, in many cases they have proven themselves legitimate with actual journalism between the editorial nonsense. Fox's Journalistic integrity usually comes with a soon to be disproved right wing slant or carefully chosen twists of context sporting a large measure of purposefully disingenuous intensity.

[FOCAL POINT:
Think about that in the big picture and what it could possibly mean to America.
A complete fringe "News" industry bent with political prejudices and social skews, tailor made for the disillusioned on both ends of any issue. FOR PROFIT.]

"How do you feel?... Oh, well let me tell you who did it to you and how they will do it to you next, right after you watch this message from our sponsors."
"You know, one of these new ____ inserted correctly can relieve a lot of the stress brought on by your political woes... and now back to your political woes."

Many Americans are completely happy getting their measure of politics this way. Huge money is what it means for high drama news outlets. Lack of focus and continuing feelings of inadequacy is what America gets.

We Americans used to be able to trust our news, it was a loss-leader for the networks, no money was involved. But today, pseudo-news is completely fine by every social and legal measure. Yet, somehow this scenario has the feel of being the opposite of Patriotism doesn't it? It does to me. Pitting one group of Americans against another for profit, Americans with guns.

Our own polling industry tells us that a huge percentage of Americans are disillusioned politically, socially and monetarily, equating to a big bag of money for those buying and selling ad space. You know who they are, those companies practicing their own brand of control via the media to get you to spend your last pennies on their products. Many just "pop-up," everywhere we look, by means of the fun electronics we are sold.

If we feel that we must stay minute-to-minute informed of the world's goings on, we could all start a little change in our own lives by watching unbiased news on PBS and BBC world news. Of-course, we wouldn't get that daily dose of placebo vindication to satisfy our point of view. But our lives would slowly change as we get used to news delivered without a disingenuous slant or urgent tone. Unfortunately, fewer commercials on these broadcasts also means fewer ideas on what to have for dinner. I don't mean to sound sarcastic, but this level of angst always comes out of me when I see purposeful control mechanisms in our society. Most are being used to guide us to spend money but the results are; that we are being separated as Americans into different factions of disgruntled Americans.
As far as I'm concerned, it's not right, and should not be allowed.

Another something that makes me shake my head, is the gun lobby and "news" machine that perpetuates the mindset, accepted by many paranoid Americans, that their government is coming to take their guns. These are the type of people that have a gun at every turn in their lives to protect themselves against such an incursion.

I have researched firearms and the people that use them, *and* the results, from people to government, for six solid years now, and I have seen no serious evidence of this at all. Yet this idea persists and is turned into mob mentality whenever any angle or thought of firearms is brought up for discussion. This idea facilitates unlocked guns, and a paranoid, hair trigger mindset.

These people's free, human lives, are being stunted by the fear that money and power have created under the guise of "American Values," and "Freedom of Choice."

How many of us have left the country and observed how the rest of the world lives? How many of us have seen for ourselves, the happiness others in our world have, even though they aren't Americans? This is a great freedom afforded to us as Americans, a real-life education in humanity, actual, tangible Liberty. Unfortunately, many of us seldom travel. Some, being so obsessed with guns, they can't bring themselves to go anywhere simply because they can't have the security they feel a gun provides them. Some never go far from home at all. Their favorite news channel has them thinking that people are waiting to kill them at every turn.

I say, America has failed if we can't make our people feel safe in their homeland without feeling the need for a gun every time they look outside. Ugh.

Do you want to know another little piece of human nature? A piece that can minimize these others that I've just gone over? A need for belonging and purpose, *Solidarity.*

Solidarity is realized as people come together to champion a common cause. Americans should have solidarity as a country but we don't anymore, Capitalism has effectively taken that from us. The pro-gun movement has a very loose knit solidarity that has many chinks in its armor. The guns at any cost crowd are melded with the "Constitutionalist" crowd with the "just want a gun" crowd, among other pro splinter groups.

All having different reasons, and levels of need and want for firearms, a sort of blind solidarity.

Solidarity is a great part of human nature, but blind solidarity is malleable and must be nurtured with thought. The pro-gun solidarity in the United States will inevitably be shunned in the favor of strict gun control if positive steps aren't soon taken.

"*Why*?" Because both Death *and* Love, trumps them all.

Example:
When we kill one al-Qaida terrorist, we create ten more that knew and loved that person, we have proven it. These ten didn't necessarily see that terrorist person as a terrorist or even believe in their tenets as a terrorist. They first saw that person as a family member or loved one. When we killed that person, their friends and family became enraged and consequently converted to a terrorist way of thought. They want revenge out of human nature. Effectively, by killing one terrorist, we created ten. **- End**

This is the situation we have here in the United States. Merely replace the word terrorist with "gun violence victim," and you may start to realize what is now happening in our country.

With every gun violence victim, with every gun violence survivor, we create at least ten more people *(via social media perhaps even more)* that are now soured on the idea of any type of gun. Of-course there are also those non-gun owners whose paranoia is stoked and then go out and buy a gun, but only a few in comparison. Those that go out and buy a gun under these conditions aren't actual gun people, they have just become scared to the point of negative action. Their thoughts will change back if given a positive chance. In the mean-time, these new gun owners have little training or ability, just paranoia. So, we have possibly then created a few more gun dangerous situations to wade through.

If you call to the past for your answers, go ahead, explore. It's all true. How did the United States even come into existence? With every instance of Royal oppression more and more people became aware until they took action and left England in hopes of a better life. When this oppression continued, we separated ourselves from that oppression.

It's human nature to move away from negativity. It is also human nature to dig-in and be an obstinate whipping post. Which are you?

Manipulation, Hyperbole, Lie, Cheat, Steal, Pander and Kill.

It's all human nature and completely explainable, but fixable or manageable for our purpose under our system of free-for-all Capitalism is a whole different issue.

What a mess we have here, and in the closet is a loaded and unlocked gun.

"Why did you sting me? The Frog asked the scorpion...."

Ok, here it is.

I imagine, if you haven't already jumped ahead and read this chapter, a few people might be waiting to read my ideas on our Second Amendment.

First, I'd like to mention that I don't think our firearms issue can be addressed from the Second Amendment angle but I do think that we should think about the Second Amendment on its own. I address the Second Amendment here mainly because it is expected in a discussion such as this, and the angle I will address, needs to have its own respect for the Second Amendment.

Secondly, I am not a Constitutional Scholar, nor have I had any formal training in the field. What I am is a relatively intelligent American citizen. The same kind of American that was urged to consider the new Constitution by what are now called the Federalist Papers. These were arguments and explanations for our Constitution, intended for the normal rational people of the 1780's.

We rational, educated people of the 21st Century, can surely contemplate these early founding documents at the level of that day. And what's better is, that today, we have the benefit of history, hindsight, modern morals and current world conditions as angles to see them from.

Over the years and up to just recently, I have read and contemplated many of our Country's founding documents. I have found them amazingly visionary for the time in which they were enacted and still heartening today.

American Druthers

- The Second Amendment -

Among the angles of thought on how our guns are used in America, is why our attitude and entitlement in relation to our firearms has morphed. Through the years, our attitude has come to include bits and pieces of want, based loosely in current modern situations. We are clinging to ideas that weren't included in the original meanings, causes and uses of our country's Constitution so many years ago. Because no discussion on the subject of guns in America would be complete, or valid without a mention, let's explore the Second Amendment to our Constitution. But more than that, let us look at this piece of our heritage from as many angles as we can imagine.
Let us discuss and dissect it.

"A well regulated militia, being necessary to the security of a free state, the right of the people to keep and bear arms shall not be infringed."

This is the exact wording of, *"Amendment II"* to the Constitution of the United States of America.
It is not really very long, a mere twenty-seven words. Penned, championed and offered to the original Continental Congress by James Madison, one of our founding Fathers, and our fourth U.S. President. In our American microcosm, this offering has perhaps become the most controversial string of words ever put together by humans for consideration.
It's right up there with, "Thou Shalt Not Kill."

I am more than sure that most gun owners don't know these exact words. Yet, if asked how many people do I think claim to live by these words and call to them on a regular basis, blindly standing behind these words to protect their personal esteem, I would have to say "most gun owners," again.

It's only one sentence, and surprisingly simple. It even starts to roll off the tongue when you try and memorize it. This fact being good for us here in this discussion because the first part to exploring these twenty-seven measly words, is to memorize them front to back. Any mother hugger that wants to go toe to toe, better be able to state these words upside down and backwards, with a proper understanding of the context, and English language they were written in.
Explore your own feelings on these words. Is it the ideal they represent, the mob mentality they incite, or the words themselves that give you a right?
If you are serious about this cause, you should have these twenty-seven words down pat to start with. If you own a gun and call to these words as your way of life, you better damn well know them, otherwise... shut your face.
But of course, knowing the Second Amendment by memory doesn't make any one person's argument more important than another's. It's merely the base from where we all start. It is a bare necessity and the least common denominator to the discussion at hand.
You need to start off by at least knowing what the hell you're talking about. For chrysakes, membership to the Cub Scouts of America used to require the ability to recite the Cub Scout promise, and it strangely enough, was also twenty-seven words. As a matter of fact, a Cub Scout had to be able to dissect their little memorized spiel and discuss its parts meanings. Hhmm... the Cub Scout promise was retired and replaced...

Not seriously comparing similarities or anything, just sayin'.

As with all parts of the United States Constitution, the parts within are ideas. Ideas that were once batted around and through need and substance, at some point put on paper (velum) as intended practice for the people of our new country.

So what is an amendment? The word amendment at its core means to change. Webster's Dictionary of the English language defines it as such...

Amend: (the root word)
1) To change some of the words and often the meaning of a document, law, etc. 2) To change and improve something such as a mistake or a situation.

Amendment:
1) A change in the words or meaning of a law or document such as a Constitution. 2) The act or process of changing the words or meaning of a law or document. The act or process of amending something.

I have heard the argument that our founders were using the word amendment as the word "addition." I'm not sure why that would make a difference other than to argue over semantics, or to remove the word "change" from the definition, but I personally don't think this was the case. They took more pride in language back then than we do today. Our forefathers were, if nothing else, painstakingly adept at the English language. They had the word "addition" in their vocabularies as well as other words with similar meanings and chose not to use them. I do realize that "amendment," is one of these synonyms also but then if we must explore further, we defer to its Georgian English use. This is a point of thought for this discussion; Language etymology and the changes in our English language in the last 250 years. An important angle to explore considering that even today the English language morphs before our eyes. In every generation since our founder's days, our English language has been re-defined in many ways.

Words are not steadfast, they morph and change as the environment they are used in changes. The Webster dictionary adds and subtracts words annually as well as adding definitions to older words to fit current uses. Ask a true Englishman today, is there a difference between the English language and American English? There are even points in time used to display these changes in English. Georgian English, Victorian era, etc.

As a matter of fact, all of our nation's founding documents took a very long time to finish in part because of the arguments brought forth in relation to context, words and their meanings to different people within the original colonies. Our founders used a Samuel Johnson Dictionary, and we can look through this same 1785 edition today for comparison to modern definition. These men took the time to get this article correct for their intent as a new free nation in the late 1700's.

The very fact that there are amendments to these documents is proof in of itself that our country's forefathers had second thought. They obviously looked around and thought that the situations at hand needed further definition to their cause. This has been quite common throughout our country's history as our laws of governance in the United States have in some instances been amended and in others repealed on a regular basis. This cannot be denied as these facts are written in volumes of public record both at the Federal and State levels throughout the United States. I don't really need to add examples of this as means, anyone can look these things up on the internet.

I personally feel that the man that wrote the Second Amendment is purposefully kept in the background and rarely talked about. The Second Amendment is largely the brain child of just one man, James Madison. If we were to ask Second Amendment supporters about James Madison, I wonder how many even know he is responsible for this piece of our heritage. He is also primarily responsible for verbiage of similar intent in the Constitutions body.

If we look back on James Madison's life, both thought and action, we can get a little background and a more clear idea for the need and intent of the Second Amendment.

James Madison: micro-bio

Princeton Graduate with emphasis on speech and debate, according to his biographer, was "immersed in the liberalism of enlightenment."

Oversaw his local Virginia Militia during the Revolutionary War.

Wrote the "Virginia Plan," which became the first drafts of our United States Constitution, endowing him with the title of "Father of the Constitution."

Co-wrote The Federalist Papers.

Sponsored the Bill of Rights, and among others, offered up our Second Amendment for review.

Co-Founded the Democratic Republican party.

Served as U.S. Secretary of State from 1801 to 1809.

Served as our fourth U.S. President from 1809 to 1817.

Famously said;

- *"If men were Angels, no government would be necessary."*

- *"Knowledge will forever govern ignorance; and a people that mean to be their own governors, must arm themselves with the power which knowledge gives."*

From his biography, I see James Madison as a highly educated, thinking man of action. During the Revolutionary War, he saw more bloodshed than is imaginable today. And all of his efforts were against monarchies and invaders, signs of the times he lived in. The Americas were breaking free from Europe and supporting others doing the same.

James Madison was also a vocal proponent of free American higher education and hospital surgeries. Most of his ideas other than those based in physical protection are not included in the current conservative political handbook.

As a matter of fact, James Madison was of a progressive liberal mindset. Remember, firearms from the state of having none and them being a device of class and religion, to all people having one was a progressively liberal idea back then.

What was the reasoning behind James Madison's penning of the Second Amendment to our Constitution? Why did our other leaders agree?
Did our founding fathers want to give us the idea that the Americans around us are our enemies and must be threatened at all times to keep from killing us? Was it that material goods are equal to human life and we need guns to kill those that threaten those goods? I personally don't think this was the case by any stretch of the imagination.
From his full life's biography, I would say that his intent was to ensure that America didn't turn out like England. He wanted to ensure that the people of the Americas were ready to fight man by man to maintain their new homeland, and in the end, couldn't be oppressed by the strength of their own government, such as it was in the late 1700's.

The United States has set precedent time and time again by changing our governance to suit our ever-evolving ways of American thinking, and ever-changing world environment. The fact and practice of amendments to the United States Constitution lends credence to the ideals of change within America. In fact, the people of the thirteen original colonies and their newly formed Constitutional Government took these brave steps in part to throw off the shackles of governance without evolutionary change.

Since these early days of American example, the entire world has
sped up, due primarily to the attitudes of change that we as
Americans held, and currently hold dear. Personal freedoms
were a radical change from the world order back in the 1700's.
The world has not evolved at such a speed in known history as it
has since the inception of the United States Constitution. This
document of ours has affected the entire world.
Unfortunately, in some ways, we as Americans have done our
best since those days to prove the old ways correct. The old ways
that were based on the idea that most people left to their own
devices are a detriment to themselves and others, therefore in
need of control. In America we have many freedoms. Among
these is to decide what is or isn't to our detriment. This is often
to our own detriment, to spite others and way out of anyone's
immediate control.

Back in the heyday of the American Revolution, the land mass
known as the Americas was wild and untamed. Exploration of
these lands was spotty, and people of these days were much
more in tune to their environment than we are today.
They lived under conditions of life hard to even imagine with
true understanding today, in our world of instant travel and
immediate gratification. I would guess, of the 320+ million
people within the boundaries of the United States, there may
actually be less than a few million that can stand the prolonged
gore and blood-letting that was a necessity and daily occurrence
in 1789 when the United States Constitution was new. The
entirety of the new country with its colonies had a population of
less than three million people, way less. In contrast, that is about
how many people live in just the Boston Massachusetts area
today.
In those days education of our world was also spotty. Not only of
who became educated, but how much education they got, and
what this education consisted of. The content of education in
those days could of course only include the known world and the

known issues and sciences up to that point.

Today, we know infinitely more on every subject of the world around us. Today, a person with a Doctorate Degree in the sciences has perhaps a hundred times more knowledge than a lifetime scholar of the 1780's could have ever hoped for. Truly, a person in today's world with an above average intellect and a Bachelor's degree, has more book knowledge on most subjects than the top ten percent of the world's scholars on the same subject at the time of our Revolution. Strange to think in those terms, but undeniably true.

If we discuss *life knowledge*, which is an entirely different subject, today, we here in the United States know very little in comparison to our forefathers. We now actually know less on this subject than most of the rest of the world. These early Americans lived off the land and traveled by muscle driven determination. In comparison, we today are a bunch of whining, overweight freshmen. They used rudimentary tools, lived their lives largely by superstition and overcame obstacles by general consensus. They knew little of the entire worlds workings, and when reading or socializing in the evening, it was by candle light. Using that same candle to see while using a bedpan or outhouse toilet in the yard for midnight relief. Crazily enough, our first President, George Washington, died of quackery. Our best doctors bled him to death with leeches. That's just how far removed from today those people were back then. There is no place on Earth left for us to wander, so it is very hard for us to understand the way those brave people felt in this open land alone. One of the rudimentary tools they used for their survival was in its infancy of evolution at the time, but never the less, helped to provide food for the table and was a step-up from sharpened steel as a means of protection. The flintlock and/or percussion cap firearm, at that point in time, was nothing more than a hand held cannon of questionable accuracy and reliability.

Cumbersome, in both size and weight, it was able to shoot once, then took a minute, more-or-less to re-load. Under fighting conditions, it was usually fired once in a unison volley then used as a battering ram or spear if fitted with a bayonet. Although laughable by today's standards, this was the high technology of that day. All men in the colonies were expected to at least know how to use one if called upon to provide food or protection. It was a life's basic necessity in the early years of our free country. With such a rudimentary tool for these uses we can all surely understand the need in those times and its relation to the Second Amendment. It was truly an instrument needed and used in the 1700's for survival of the fittest.

Fast forward to today in our modern age.
We have more than 320 million people within the United States boundaries compared to the roughly 2.5 million in 1780, *and* the world's most powerful military. We no longer have the basic need for defense of our ideal's person by person with firearms. Today, unfortunately we perceive the real need to protect ourselves *from each other* with firearms.
I think this perception, believe it or not, stems from Capitalism and Materialism, two ideals that hadn't quite taken hold in the 1700's the way we address them today. It stems from lack of education and low self-esteem. It stems from over population and material excess. It is a symptom of our conditioning. And we continue to negatively program ourselves with the violence we have created for profit and entertainment all around us.

Back in the 1700's death was more common to the average American, blood and guts were everyday fare. If you wanted meat on the table, you had to spill blood yourself. Today we don't realize how fragile we really are underneath our egos, desensitized to the fact that we ourselves are blood and guts. We as Americans collectively think that because those people struggled and won, that we are somehow deserving.

We have a long standing entitlement to our guns, but as "overweight freshmen," we can't keep pointing to the Second Amendment with a straight face knowing its core intent no longer applies. The only constant in our world is change and we have come to a point where America once again, needs to evolve.

The Second Amendment is actually pretty clear in its intent when you tear it apart, but as for its current viability, not yet held to the same standards we hold other parts of the constitution to for today's realities. To take the attitude that this was written as a decree for all time is ludicrous and exceedingly shortsighted. Ideas like these are no more than arguments brought forth to selfishly quell human advancement.
The idea that the men that wrote this were beyond reproach is also not a very smart angle since the internet can once again point you to the biographies of each man that had a hand in its manufacture. These men were all Patriots to the American cause with many selfish reasons included in their interpretations of the word "Freedom." I challenge you to come up with a single man that enacted the Declaration of Independence or U.S. Constitution without a closet full of skeletons or even morals that meet our modern standards… not one will you find.
These were the smartest men we had. The brightest available, but by today's standards they are merely the prettiest girls in the room. These men would go completely berserk if they had to make the same decisions they made then, under the conditions of our day. I speculate if they had to make these same decisions in today's environment the results would be a bit more than *slightly* different. The word "stroke," comes to mind.

I'm going to print the wording here again on the next page so that we all don't have to keep flipping back so far. If you still haven't memorized it, please take some time and do so.

"A well regulated militia, being necessary to the security of a free state, the right of the people to keep and bear arms shall not be infringed."

We've looked at these words from a historical viewpoint. Really, a place from where most truth comes, the origin. How we interpret and implement this truth in our modern time is where we now stumble.

Since we know they went to great pains for succinct meaning, leaving out much of the fluff common in Georgian English prose, we can stand with these men. We can now look back to their place and time to empathize with their cause.

I've seen the Second Amendment itself broken into three pieces by placement of the commas or two pieces by placement of *perceived* intent, divided only at the second comma. I personally like the three-piece method because commas give little breaks in sentences to help separate ideas.

"A well regulated militia,"

As previously mentioned, these were intelligent men and men with urgent purpose. We know they were thinking of the future as much as they could imagine it to be. Being human beings themselves, we can figure that none of them could see any further into the future, or imagine any more of how things might be 250 years from then, than you or I can right now at this very moment, imagine with any accuracy, what the earth will be like 250 years from now. It stands to reason, especially when you consider their state of science.

Certainly, they knew the differences between the words "Militia" and "Army." They were, after-all, fighting against England's Royal Armies. Then, as well as today, militia is the term used to describe a force of the people, as opposed to the days Aristocracy or Dictator based Government's assembled hordes of force.

In those days, in England, you were enlisted into the Royal Armies by decree. If you didn't comply, you were facing death or imprisonment.

A "well regulated" bit of anything in the Georgian era meant complete and not wanting, well taken care of. In the Georgian English vernacular of that day a well-regulated militia included being well funded, it included being well staffed, it meant a strictness of structure. A word in itself with several intertwined principle meanings being conveyed all at once.

Pretty effin' smart, with the first four words they convey several instructions at once. It's what I'd expect from these guys though, they were after all, the prettiest girls in the room.

"being necessary to the security of a free state,"

Here, they are acknowledging need, and making clear once again, as in the main document itself, they consider the need based in their separation as independent and free.

All of them together (the Colonies) as one state of being, one state in purpose as a "United State," against any invading factions at hand.

Very Cool, in a modern translation of wording we could say; "Our armies made up from our people will be as good as absolutely possible to secure and protect the United States."

The word "free" in those days meant different things to different people, depending on status, religion and country of origin. Freedom in the Georgian sense was so much sweeter than we can imagine today in that fewer could even hope to enjoy it. This word combined the feelings of what it meant to each one that dreamt it, into one word that people could feel when thought of or even uttered. The word "Freedom" is an example of being one of the strongest and most powerful words in all languages on Earth, stronger than any weapon, or circle of time. Throughout the ages, humans have dreamt, fought, and died for freedom.

Today, it is a shame that the word "freedom" has been reduced to an advertising slogan urging our need for high-speed internet and satellite TV.

As the advertising states, we are always free to choose.

For these reasons, I won't address the word "free," here. Mainly because today we have no real idea of freedom as the people in those times saw it. It is enough to say that we can pretty much all agree, that in some form, in everyone's mind, the United States Means Freedom. I love it.

"...the right of the people to keep and bear arms shall not be infringed."

Hot Damn Right, setting a "Right" as an American citizen right there. As an American, as in *the people*, the people in the United States. We can have and hold Arms.

We can own guns plain and simple. And by the way... don't screw with that. Don't try to take the right to own guns from us. Do nothing negating our ability as the people, as Americans, to own a gun... or two-ish, more or less.

Dammit, we can call ourselves collectors of firearms and try to get "one" of every piece of spitting steel that's ever been thought up if we want to, Hot Damn right.

The entire Second Amendment discussion hinges right here on the word infringement. It turns out, this word had, and has, a very broad meaning. The United States Government itself, as well as the people that challenge, will never be able to get past the core intent of this meaning. Not because of the word itself, but because the core of our mettle as Americans has been built on the idea that we as Americans, and equally those in the rest of the world, know that invasion of American sovereign land would be futile. With this knowledge, the United States ranks supreme in the world as long as our guns are bigger and more wide spread, as long as we aren't "infringed." Guns feed not only our individual ego but our collective American ego as well.

I doubt we would ever allow this to be changed.

The only stumbling block to understanding in this section as far as I can tell, would be the word "people." Because of course, all people aren't the same.
The only thing that "we the people" really have in common in this country is the word "American," otherwise we are as different as every snowflake in the desert.
The People... the Americans.

Who are Americans?
Are Americans adolescent dumbasses?
Yes, in some cases they are.
Are Americans violent?
Yes, in some cases they are.
Are Americans mentally ill?
Yes, in some cases they are all of these things.

Americans of questionable competency are also being spoken of here in our Second Amendment and up until this very day, we are all ok with that.
There are many classifications of who and what Americans are. We can easily say that the word "American," and the word used in the Second Amendment "people," are synonymous.
So, if Americans are sometimes mentally ill, is it ok to give them a gun? Should we walk into a mental institution and pass out our old revolvers? Make sure they have one in the nightstand?
In this case, what is the difference between a mentally ill American locked away and one still roaming the streets?
Nothing. The issue isn't whether they have already hurt someone or whether they have been caught hurting themselves or others. No, the issue is that they have a diminished mental capacity making it dangerous to allow them a killing machine. That is the core reason, the rest is the consequence. If they don't use it themselves will they allow someone else to use it through neglect?

I don't want to imply that all mentally ill people are murderous or suicidal though, most are not. That is, most of those that have been diagnosed are not. Mental illness is on a grand sliding scale including nuances that have nothing to do with our discussion here. Emotional illnesses are also bunched in with mental illness along with those pushed over the edge by drugs and abuse. I dare say that there are *a lot* more undiagnosed issues walking the streets with guns in America than there are people diagnosed. The problem with that being, we make our judgements and policies based on those diagnosed numbers. I'll bet most of us can come up with uncomfortable instances in our lives involving mentally or emotionally disturbed people and certain people we personally know that perhaps shouldn't be allowed to own a killing device such as a gun.

In all the uproar surrounding each gun violence incident here in the U.S., I haven't actually heard much about taking guns away from the people. Not even now, 2000+ mass shootings since my own *lesser* incident.

What I've heard primarily, is of proposed owner restrictions and types of guns not needed by the public. It always turns into one side arguing for owner restrictions and the other yelling someone is trying to take their guns.

Point being, the Second Amendment doesn't say we can have any gun we want. I'd go as far as saying plural is included but as far as our founders having any idea when approving the Second Amendment of what we are capable of today... It is an absolute impossibility that they could fathom a dream in finite particle of what the science of expanding gas has become or even what our volatile modern environment has become. Just because an old Browning .50 caliber automatic machine gun is defined as a gun doesn't mean we should all get to own one. This would be the self-serving argument of an un-aware person. Of course, some of us here in America *can* own one of these monstrosities, those of us that have the proper training, credentials and have been

screened. We certainly have no real *need* for one. If it comes down to it, we have bigger guns available at our local National Guard Armories. If we all need to get together to thwart the aggressors, that's where our society keeps our big guns.
At the very least, I think we can all agree that the Second Amendment is about need, not want.

But all that sounds very left handed doesn't it? That's why I always strive to remember;
"Guns don't kill people, People kill people."
As we have discussed, this is obviously true. But there is another angle to be seen.
As we address our Second Amendment, we can all notice that it does not address issues of public safety, neither does any part of our Constitution. At that point in time there was no need. I can only imagine that our founders felt our solidarity as Americans was a glue that would hold us together, that we would always, at the very least, respect each other as countrymen.

We can all see that with our population and current collective states of being, policing the people in the United States from an angle of public safety is something that comes to mind when so many people are being needlessly shot and killed on a daily basis. The CDC in the United States considers our growing gun violence epidemic a public safety issue. And after my own study and personal experience, I can do nothing but agree. It's people we have to worry about, not necessarily the guns. We have a lot of people in this country now, and with larger gross numbers of good people, come larger gross numbers of bad people.
It is time to bring a little peace of mind to the good people on both sides of this topic.

You may have taken a little bit of an emotional rollercoaster through this chapter as you tried to pin me down on whether I am for, or against, the Second Amendment.

Plain and simple, I am for the intent of the Second Amendment but against the crutch for complacency it has become in our modern age. It no longer applies to our modern lives in a comparable fashion to when it was penned. The primary reason we have such an affinity for guns today, is out of fear of guns themselves, and some of the people we allow to use them.
Our courts have studied and rejected several challenges to the Second Amendment over time. Each argument coming from a slightly different angle as to challenge its current validity. That hasn't worked well, and most likely never will.

We are in a desperate time. There has never been a time in our history when there has been as much infighting as there is today. All types of shootings have been steadily going up. We could have started paying attention with the St. Valentine's day murders that sparked a huge public outcry. The gun fervor after John F. Kennedy and Martin Luther King's killings in the 1960's didn't do anything. If the nearly Seventy Thousand Americans being shot every year from gun violence doesn't shake us, we are way too jaded. If the fact that our friends and family are on the short list to death and injury each day as they go to school or work doesn't wake us up, we may be hopeless.

I submit without reservation, that the firearms issue in the United States has nothing to do with the Second Amendment. Our problem with guns is actually with the people using them, making this an issue of public safety. Our firearms laws should be fashioned for the vetting and culling of dangerous minds, all the while keeping the Second Amendment in mind.
In spite of the Second Amendment, we will choose either the freedom to live or the freedom to die. The easiest version to claim is the freedom to die, the way we currently experience our lives. Sit by, do nothing. Afraid of the next phone call, living scared of those around us... the Americans around us. The harder way, is to change, nothing easy is worthwhile.
We used to know this without being told.

At twelve we saw it as so much fun
At twenty we have way more than one
At thirty we see the damage we've done
At forty we worry because now it's our son
To make the hard choices
To do the right thing
To live by the gun we feel a dull sting
Now as you ponder on what we have done
Your child has been killed by a nut with a gun

Mac/

American Druthers

- Need vs. Want -

Have you ever thought about how these two words relate to each other? Want stems from need but want comes from other places also. A person can want something for many reasons but the word "need," imparts an urgency to the subject. Need is a definition of something you must have to start, continue, or finish everything. Need is all around us. We need air, we need water, we need food, and many other things to sustain life. There are the things that we need for comfort. Things like homes and cars and a full mouth of teeth. Then there are things we need to maintain ourselves as human beings, like affection, goals and mental stimulation of all kinds. There are also many things we might personally need that others don't, but we can all separate the things in our lives pretty much into these two categories of want and need.

Most of the world can see the basic flaw in the American Capitalist model and they complain about it constantly. Many of our country's "friends" and neighbors aren't even sure they like us, they merely accept our control under fear of sanction. Other countries are directly on our heels, ready to follow us to oblivion or wherever we lead them. Capitalism has skewed our American thinking, and consequently those that follow us, into a twisted and mangled materialistic society where shiny monetary baubles have an equal standing with humanity.
What's more; our social sciences have advanced to the point we can sell anything to anyone. You don't have to be a psychology major or an advertising executive to control people into buying or selling. Those skills can be had at the associate levels. We can make anyone with eyes, ears or a nose…. want.

America has become the manipulative bastard stepchild of the world, enjoying our excesses while they last, then tossing the empties in anyone's bed to sleep on. We even have an entire political industry devoted to selling and buying.

If we discover a shiny button that snaps to tie, we Americans will soon have built an entire industrial monolith to service this idea complete with marketing, lobbyists and black-market knockoffs. So when we decide to fight an issue in the United States, we aren't fighting just an issue, we are fighting what we have built up around this issue to sell it. We are having to fight our capitalist mindset and the marketing we've instilled via our psychological manipulations. We have now proudly devised a system that takes about seventy-five years to sell us everything a good American "*needs*" to have before their funeral makes room for another customer.

It seems the only reason we care if you die is that you will no longer be able to buy our stuff... Oh, never mind, your kids just bought two in memory, go ahead, Croak.

What I'm saying here is, let's ponder the meaning of the words "need," and "want," as they apply to our discussion without thinking that one substitutes for the other. It's not to our advantage to meld the meanings of these words. It helps when selling things to each other but in politics it is a definite stumbling block. Politics need to be based in a defined, forward thinking reality to work. To explore need in the manner we are discussing it here, first we must set a constant then decide what we *need* to maintain that constant. For this discussion our constants are spelled out for us in our country's founding documents.

Every American has the inalienable right to Life, Liberty and the Pursuit of Happiness. We may have a hard time shoving that down the necks of the rest of the world as we hold them under our thumb, but our utopian society here in America thrives on these devil-may-care ideals.

As Americans, we have come up with many things we both enjoy and can be dangerous at the same time. Cars and motorbikes for instance are some of the most sought-after items in America and people are killed by these every day. Many things can kill us in today's world, so we try to separate those into things that kill by attrition, and those that kill with human fault.

Attrition of course can't be stopped, things happen, people die and we all carry a personal responsibility to realize this. In fact, all death is attrition in the grand scheme.

When a car is used by a drunk driver to plow down a bus stop full of people, we certainly can't blame the car. Of course, it's the person driving the car that is responsible... oops, I mean the insurance company.

But if a gun was used by a person to kill those same bus patrons, the person shooting the gun would be responsible same as the driver of the car was, but likely there would be no insurance *(or even a heartfelt apology)* for the incident. This is a core problem we have with America's gun attitude. Not only do we think that we desperately need firearms, we also think that we should be absolved of any responsibility for owning them and the results of their intended or un-intended uses. Having a responsibility in relation to our killing machines is not infringement.

Plain and simple, *guns are dangerous.*

Yes, you can use a baseball bat to kill someone. Yes, you can do the same with a car. BUT... you can also play baseball and convey yourself with these items. When they aren't being misused as killing devices they are being used in a harmless manner. Their primary purpose is of innocent intent. It is also very hard to accidentally kill or maim someone with a bat or a car from a distance of more than a few feet.

The gun on the other hand has a primary purpose to kill and destroy and when misused does the same.

So where is our American concern for public safety? Our vitriol for liability, our basic human decency?

Is our American heritage about digressing as humans? Is our Constitution there to cover our asses?

America NEEDS to have every firearm owned by U.S. citizens insured for liability. Period.
I see no way around it and no viable argument that stands on its own against.
Unfortunately, the cost of each mis-used American freedom bullet, continues on to cost the rest of the country dearly.

Here's one way it goes...
A methamphetamine addict burglarizes a house and steals a gun. The meth-head soon shoots another person with the gun. The event around this drug induced shooting included destroyed property both public and private. The meth-head shooter goes to jail for fifteen years on the public dole. The public and insurance company pick up the repair bills for all the destroyed property. Chances are good that the person he shot didn't die or have adequate health insurance so the public pays that staggering hospital bill. Then once out of the hospital, the now crippled victim gets on Social Security Income, Food Stamps and Medicaid because they can no longer work.
That's roughly ten million dollars to be spent by the people of the United States to maintain two people's destroyed lives because one gun owner didn't have their gun locked away when not in use and didn't have it insured for liability.
This is the normal configuration of this tale, not the exception. This scenario, or one similar, plays out dozens of times every single day, all over the United States, every day of the year.
I've personally heard of this scenario at least a dozen times in similar slant as I've talked with other victims, and I've only talked with a miniscule percentage. It has also been part of my own experience. YOU, the American tax payer, are paying to keep my attacker in jail for as long as he's there. The American tax payer also paid for most of my hospital stay.

Who do you think pays for all of this death and destruction?

Many states have a victims of violence fund padded by the tax payer to help pay these bills. Hospital bills gone unpaid are taken off the hospitals books as loss, thus reducing their tax liability which is a loss to the American tax base. This is waste and abuse on a grand scale considering our state and federal governments are paying a piece, if not most of the bill when it comes to all of this daily American gun violence.

Remember, there are 320+ MILLION people in the U.S. now and our population is getting thicker by the hour. At this point, it can do nothing but get worse.

It's easy for many left-wingers to say that we merely *want* guns here in the United States, we don't need them.

There *are* other countries in the world that restrict all firearms and the people are happy. But I would never suggest that here in the United States. There are still viable American open country lifestyles that include guns, and I hope there always will be.

Being an American steeped in, and having explored in depth America's gun culture, I know that America does actually need its guns. America needs guns as a whole to bolster its sagging self-esteem instilled by our capitalist society to sell us things. Our American society runs on guns the same way our money has value, the same way our stock market makes money. The same way we "balance" our Federal budget.

Confidence, hyperbole, smoke and mirrors.

America's collective esteem is at stake when you talk guns.

America needs its guns to feel safe. This country was built on this ideal and guns everywhere is what lets Americans and the rest of the world know that intrusion on United States soil would be futile. We have simply become used to having this item as a security blanket of sorts and to take it away would in fact create anarchy. Everyone in America being able to own a gun is now the only thing that makes us special in the entire world...

...that's why we need them.

We have our Second Amendment entitlement as a crutch for American gun ownership but in-fact its original purpose was to mandate that we maintain an adequate fighting force for our country from our people. Something we do now with an all-volunteer military force, the strongest in the world.

The "guns at all costs" crowd need to simply come to the realization that we are very close to actual gun restrictions that will hurt. After a few more years of school or shopping mall shootings, all the red faced, yelling and spitting in the world won't hold back the tide.

If we need to maintain public safety and also need guns, then the smarter among us can surely see the need to get ahead of the subject for compromise on this issue.

Obstructionism has become a situation in the past few years that is increasingly hard to overcome. Obstructionism is what will drag us down as a country if we aren't careful, because obstructionism does not come from the people, it comes from money and big business trying to maintain their own status quo of greed at any cost. Big business' like gun manufacturers and the NRA make BILLIONS every year to keep us in guns and bullets. Every bit of the gun industry will spend as much as they need, to keep selling. The American political engine runs on this money and will stand beside this money till the last penny.

By now we all know that the only way to change this, is to remove the money. Then we run into another in depth discussion on how everything is tied to everything else in a big circle. It seems by pulling one thread, the whole issue unravels and becomes a twisted mess. That's usually where everyone stops, just staring in disbelief at what a mess the whole situation has become. We all shake our heads and walk away swearing not to give-in to the feelings of righteous indignation next time. The news cycle ends and we go on with our lives till the next. This situation is contrived to be as it is, this is purposeful. This is our want, need, and human nature being used against us.

When we get to that point of frustration, someone needs to remind us all; at this point, there will always be a next shooting down the block, across town... on national news, daily, monthly and literally by the minute. And the odds are very good that someone you know will be included, if not yourself.

So, we:
Need public Safety
Need guns in America
Need to get ahead of the issue before it rots
Need to adjust our thinking
Need to think of ways to compromise

As Americans, we need to occasionally check ourselves on the major issues of our country. Simply because we can do something, does that mean that we should?
Yes, it means we *should* think deeply before we act.
In the 21st century the world is led by thought, not by might. If you claim or believe that the past holds certain truths for the future then all you have to do is look back on how many times might has failed to thought... Always, every single time. The results of might have never been permanent, not once. You may point to WWII but there are Nazi's and the like right here in America being protected by our own Constitution. We can't kill our way to peace, we've proven it.
We claim to use our guns and the might that they give us, to champion peace throughout the world but the fact is, that since 1776 the United States has only enjoyed 14 years of *not* having an armed conflict. Fourteen years out of 243 is a sad statement for the effectiveness of guns.

Our "one-day" is coming, our one-step-over-the-line mass shooting is looming. We NEED to address this issue to try and maintain some semblance of American gun rights.

It doesn't take a rocket scientist to see that the bad apple spoiling the whole barrel effect is soon to happen to the gun loving public. The pile of rotten cores is getting larger every year. When we do finally cross that line, the slam of the door will be very loud. Some guy with a gun or two is going to go into another public space and kill a lot of people. One of the dead or directly affected will be a rich, connected, one percenter type person and the ball will start to roll faster. The outrage will have become palpable to the right people and sweeping reform will be thrust upon us. This scenario is not a guess, it is inevitable, and by not taking action to head it off, we are accepting these bleak terms. I would imagine this to happen in my children's lifetime if not headed off in some fashion.

Everything is intertwined, absolutely everything. And each part of everything has an effect that is far reaching in subliminal ways. Each miniscule effect glomming to others to create a condition that includes nuance of hate, desire, need etc. The disparity caused by capitalism has created a sub culture of down trodden who's only comfort is the power a gun gives them as a way to imagine themselves whole. This gun and the idea of the power they wield because of it, becomes part of their personality and thus guns and their future become a personal issue for these Americans bolstered by our Second Amendment entitlement.

As a country, we NEED to get past this.

Life by the gun, is there no choice?
An American ideal run amok
With violence and greed and fuzzy excuse
We sell our ideals for a buck
With hate and aggression, we hold our guns dear
An attitude we claim to abhor
But soon as it's heard there may be a stop
We'd kill you to buy even more

We claim need, but hold and bear out of fun
Yet life by the gun isn't really a life,
when you spend your life holding a gun

Mac/

American Druthers

- Goals, Not Gun Restrictions -

There has been quite a bit of off-gassing from the pages of this
book, don't you think?
It seems that every other word is *gun, firearm or blah.. blah...*
The topic is quite intense, the tone has been quite intense.

I feel America as a gun loving and gun fearing country is going
about this all wrong. We are reacting rather than preventing. For
some reason, we think that restrictions on the tool will work, but
how can that work when it's the user that is really in question?
It makes no sense.
Do you have an idea yet as to why we think and react this way?

Perhaps we should slow down and let the other side have a say.
I've been rambling on and on about the people, and have
forgotten to follow even my own advice. Let's patiently, and
compassionately, listen to what a group of guns have to say. Or
perhaps if we are lucky enough, a real big caliber gun will clatter
right up and start spewing its side of the story. Ratta-Tat-Tat
Perhaps it will entertain us with a story of its last use, or maybe a
story of another gun it might know that has actually killed...... or
threatened.... or laid there uselessly waiting for an owner to take
notice or.... rust to set in.
I can't imagine anything else a gun might say.
I can't imagine this, or anything like it, because guns can't walk,
talk or wave howdy.
We have a bit of a misnomer being perpetuated here.

We do not have a gun issue in America, we have a people issue.
Americans being disenfranchised and disillusioned by their
Government, and the Capitalism it protects, is really our issue.

You may have noticed that a theme has been rising in these pages. People think, people are smart, people are devious, people are cunning, people are many things when it comes to how they think and act in America. Sometimes it's hard to imagine another person's train of thought since other people's personalities, abilities and lives are so much different than our own. But one thing we know for absolute sure, when telling a group of humans anything that restricts....

When told no, it's not the end.

Gun restrictions will not work in any way to reduce the amount of shootings and killings in the United States.

Gun restrictions are obstruction to the real problem. They are merely a band-aid over a wound that has not been cleaned. Then we point to the wound as a two-year old would and say, "Look Mommy, fixed." We will bat the restrictions ball around just enough to piss-off more people sitting on the edge. Some restrictions will pass, some will not. As we make our American fervor worse, people will still be getting shot.
Our representatives will breathe a sigh of relief that this pacification frenzy worked. At least until the end of their next term in office.

Example:
If we proudly say that we have banned extended capacity magazines and that now, no-one else can be killed in a group of ten or more. How can we know until the next? THE NEXT WILL LIKELY HAPPEN NEXT MONTH when one of those two million, 30-round magazines that were grandfathered-in shows up. OR... just buy two semi-auto pistols with standard 9-10 round capacity and four extra, standard capacity magazines.... Same thing to a practiced shooter my friends, NO DIFFERENCE.
Banning high capacity magazines for firearms is a band-aid over a dirty wound. It does nothing to stop a person from killing other people with a gun.

What it really says; is that we are Ok with the killing, just not so many at a time please. The most it does, is to poke the mind of the person on the edge of sanity, towards a validation that the government might actually be coming for their guns.

Ok, let's say no-more Assault weapon sales.
Let's pretend… NO MORE AR-15 SALES after August 1st 2099.

You can bet there will be several versions of carnage before August first as the extremists blather on, and as the industry increases production to get as many produced as possible before that final day. As the gun obsessed jockey for position and enough money to buy ten more for themselves. As the industry corrects and changes to a different and perhaps more inhumane trick of the week.
Banning assault style weapons does nothing more than increase their price in the newly-made assault weapons black market. They are still available by the crate, since we CAN'T require that any that are currently owned be turned in. That would be taking guns from people.
We CAN'T do that.
The argument might then be; that with attrition these will float to the surface over time. But that is only true if no-more come across our sovereign borders from outside the country. Where our own gun companies will still be selling them by the crate. Some, no doubt to nefarious people paying others to smuggle them back into the States to be sold for immense profit in the newly-made assault weapons black market.

Look at the sad situation we are perpetuating in Chicago concerning shootings and murder. This City has law after law after restriction imposed on guns and owners within its CITY LIMITS. This is not working for them.
One might ask, *How come?* but isn't it obvious?
Because the same rules concerning firearms don't apply for all the land surrounding Chicago from sea to shining sea.

Because Chicago isn't surrounded with a twenty-foot fence, a buffer zone and restricted access where everyone is strip searched before entering a "gun free" city. It is foolish... no, downright stupid, to expect a blemish free apple in a barrel of rotten cores. It's not even a cogent talking point.
People think, and they are thinking that saying *no,* is not nearly good enough. They are thinking, *"That's BS, I'll just..."*

When we restrict the inanimate object from the sales end, leaving the same objects already out in the open and available nowhere else, that object becomes more desirable and all the minds focused on the restriction of that object create a web of thought as how to physically get around and legally subvert that restriction. No one can stop human thought, it must be directed without harmful control or disdain.

Example: No automatic weapons sales by U.S. Federal Law in the public realm of the United States since 1986. So, what do we do? We think about it a little while and create full auto conversion kits and bump-stocks that convert semi-automatic weapons to fully automatic by subverting the internal and external mechanics of the gun, *and* the law. Then, we have our lawyers and lobbyists grease the wheels to keep it going for a while.

Conversely, when we vet the mind to the use of that inanimate object and restrict only until vetted, we have created a packet of esteem to claim as our own. A solidarity of skill and ownership is created. We have created a pedestal of righteousness to achieve, to be an actual certified protector of all things America.
The dynamic of the situation changes from one of negative sanction to one of positive sanction. We re-define righteous gun ownership without taking peoples guns away.
When we restrict, we whack one of 10,000 moles. Up will pop its head again when we turn our back. Up will pop another equal to or worse than the last.
A vetted hierarchy of skill levels could solve a few problems.

I'll get sarcastic with myself now.
Negative Ned can sure tell us what's wrong but I don't hear him coming up with any answers....

The ideas I offer as to how to accomplish these seemingly impossible feats of juggling come later in the next chapter titled "Solutions." That's where I throw the balls up in the air. But first we have to set a goal. We can't work towards an end if there is no goal for our future. duh.
What could possibly be our goal here?

Three balls, two kittens and a running chain saw while traversing an obstacle course on a unicycle...
... would be a lofty goal.

That is very specific, and would take skills with well-honed efficiency. We here in America don't have anything close to that. I'll bet there is a performer out there that can do that, and I want to see it, but America has not set a goal for its firearms situation, juggling or otherwise.
No Goal, No Solution. The rest is just wasted busy work.

That's the way it works. That is the way it has always worked. Has anyone mentioned that?
Has anyone dared state the obvious?
Up until this very point in time, our only very loosely defined goal for quelling American gun violence has been to drag it out as long as possible, and do just enough to get the far-left to shut up for a bit longer.

Let us set a goal here in this book. A goal for America and its guns. A goal that will help us maintain public safety.
We will call this Mike's goal, since I can feel that look of derision you are giving this book right now. I know the intensity has risen a bit and things have gotten a little pointed. You needn't be a part of this speculation if you don't want, but I always recommend hearing all sides of a discussion before lopping off any heads.

Here is *my* goal:

I want all firearm owners in The United States to be highly trained, non-threatening and perfectly respectful with, and ultimately responsible for, their firearms.

At this point in time, and from where America's gun culture stands right now, that is a very tall order.

But is this really too much to ask?

- Is it too much to ask that a person that owns a killing device know how to properly and safely use that piece of machinery?
- Is it too much to ask that Americans not enthralled with firearms also not feel threatened by guns out in the open or by gun play in their vicinity?
- Is it too much to ask that a gun owner have positive control of their killing machines at all times no matter how many they own?
- Is it too much to ask that if a gun is improperly used that an actual person is held responsible and a victim's life isn't ruined mentally and financially by the incident?

No, it is not too much to ask.

In fact, it is a minimum, as far as realizing one's human's responsibility towards other humans, and even an American citizens responsibility towards their countrymen.

In the most advanced country on Earth, a country that pronounces in its own founding documents, that all men are created equal and have the right to Life, Liberty and the Pursuit of Happiness, it is surely not too much to ask.

This over-abundance of firearms and the attitudes we've bred are taking those unalienable rights of Life, Liberty and the Pursuit of Happiness away from nearly seventy thousand Americans and their families, every year.

Our own Declaration of Independence states these rights have been given to us by our creator and that Governments are created to protect these rights.

If we were talking about any other inanimate object, I'd say it sounds like a lawsuit waiting to happen.

"We cannot solve our problems with the same thinking that created them."

~ *Albert Einstein*

American Druthers

- Solutions -

It may seem quite arrogant to name a chapter in a book that explores such a broad and controversial subject, "Solutions." After-all, entire lifetimes have been spent pitching ideas, implementing plans and railing against both sides of the topic on the American gun issue. Our Government is at its wits end as to what to do, and it's no wonder, considering the money and Constitutional duties that they are stuck between.
I might think arrogance also, if I weren't me.
But, I don't actually claim to have all the answers, I'm sure there are angles that I overlook. But as far as thought and exploration on the subject goes, I'm your man if you'd like the truth wrapped in something other than a bloody hundred-dollar bill.
No, I don't have all the answers, but I do have a few ideas and angles of thought that could eventually turn into answers.
It is what I have to offer after my experience, and a damn sight more tempered than what we're getting from anywhere else.

Most angles of thought on this subject agree, violence with a gun is really just a symptom of our problem. We have explored the causes, and now let's see if we can place blocks in the road to keep sane, law abiding Americans armed for peaceable sporting and protection use. If it's true that people kill, and not the guns themselves, then it follows that our laws should be geared towards the training and screening of American gun owners. How and why people aren't able to realize this is the real issue. Solutions are what we need, but not only solutions to issues at hand but solutions to obstructionism of the means for change we've created and nurtured within our ranks specifically for issues such as these.

It is very important to distinguish the intent of these ideas from the hyperbole that will surround them, and realize that this topic permeates all levels in our society. It includes ALL Americans, not any one group of Americans. This is not a right or left issue, this is not a Democrat or Republican issue, this is a "safety of our American families," mainstream issue.

"Debate, Compromise and Concession," means that we talk respectfully to each other about a topic and come to an acceptable middle ground. Each side, no matter how many sides there are, most likely will have to give up a little something to make a compromise work. But first we'll have to create a framework to work within. A means of rule to help us filter our ideas together with the end result being acceptable to all sides.

So far all we have been getting is; *Why should we even worry about the bleeding-heart segments of our population? We already have a living situation here in the U.S. plenty of people are happy with, and have the right to be, Second Amendment says so.*

Again, not a quote from anyone specific, just the default idea being presented.
The answer to that attitude, as we have discussed, is that there are more people in the U.S. than our Constitution's framers ever imagined and firearms are becoming a problem for the public at large, plain and simple. I'm more than sure that we as a society aren't going to move backwards on this issue, so that leaves us with...Hmm, a means of Debate, Concession and Compromise. Where are our pretty girls? The ones with actual debate skills and reverence for our heritage? Somehow it seems familiar that we already have a system like this setup to use. But *that system* has become rendered basically useless via our good friend Capitalism. Right now, it seems our government has been permanently stained by money and power. Still standing, but useless to govern without favoring any one group of people. Right now, any group with enough money gets favored.

One of the few things we need government for; is to define the issues that people are free to decide for themselves and those issues which are a detriment to the people as a whole (laws). That is now largely for sale via the lobby industry and a lawmaker's furthest loyal relative. Money has effectively negated our governments worth.

Polls in 2013 after the Sandy Hook school shooting in 2012, showed that a majority of the people in the U.S. favored some sort of owner control of guns But money was poured in to the appropriate political funds by "big interest," and we have no difference in our situation now, some eight years later. Did I mention that as of the writing of this book, there have been over 2000 mass shootings in the US since the Sandy Hook School shooting? Not to mention the literally tens of thousands of those Americans that have been killed and shot in lesser incidents. All of this death and mayhem, for all these years, and our representatives just stare at each other.
Would you like a solution for this? It means you will have to pay attention to what is going on politically around you though.

Here are three things that would get the attention of our stodgy representatives.

Aggressively back any legislation or political upstart that champions term limits for our representatives, both Senate and Congress.
Setting term limits helps to ensure their attention to their job. No need for endless re-election contributions from big business. Makes room for new ideas and fresh people. Clears out the clutter of old ideas that have gridlocked our most important issues.

Aggressively back any legislation or political upstart that champions any lobby busting ideas.
The lobby industry is how the people of the United States are most often abused politically.

Lobbyists contribute and buy their way in to the legislative inner circles. Regular Americans have no avenue for this kind of attention. It is unfair and patently unbalanced as a governing system when money from large donors controls the thought of our representatives.

Aggressively back any legislation or political upstart that not only wants to stop gerrymandering, but also champions re-districting every state in an equal representation fashion. *Representatives from wealthier districts tend to follow the money of their wealthiest constituents with their thought and representation. These of course tend to be policies that favor the wealthy humans and corporations in their districts.*

These three things being changed in our governance will help to shift the power back to the people and push money out. Personally, I think that completely getting rid of the lobby industry would be a solution to many of our political problems. Each company could have an office of Governmental Issue. One person, in an office with a phone and a list of numbers. The same level of access to representation every other American has. Remember, the only way to change the situation we are in politically is to take away the influences of money. Corporations would have to depend on quality and value to sell their products rather than manipulating our legislation with their money.

It might also be worth mentioning, that none of these three ideas has much chance of coming to pass under our current system. Our current system lets our legislators control these points and why would they change them when they have deep corporate pockets to pick through?

Right now, I'd settle for any legislation that tamps down the gun industry. That is what's on my mind right now. A decent and basic mark for legislation to meet right now might be the idea that nothing one individual or by extension, any Corporation can do, (being considered a person) shall cause, or be the root of death or bodily injury to another.

This idea being an extension of every persons right to live and die of their own means. No manipulation, no prodding, no disingenuous portrayal. Seems pretty straight forward to me, but we fail on these points time after time.
I think everyone can agree that this is a basic moral right.

What is seemingly good, is that humanity has advanced to the point that we can realistically strive for ends to help ensure this right to everyone, at least here in America. We have the ability to do all of this, but lack the attention span to pull it off. We have too many shiny things to buy and retirements to fund.

Another topic to consider while exploring the big picture is extremism. This is a danger to progress at many levels and is a losing proposition for all involved. All we have to do is look back in history to find what happens to extreme points of view. Extremists never win at anything. The best they can hope for is for their failure to come slowly. All they really do, is dull the argument of their closest constituent base, enough for everything they stand for as a whole, to be negated in favor of those less tainted. It amazes me that they can't see that effect to start with but still, there is more extremist nonsense at every turn. Extremism is at its core, the epitome of selfishness. The very idea that you and yours have the *unquestionable* answers to the issues at hand and everyone must conform to them is absolutely ignorant and has little hope of keeping thinking people's attention for very long.

Extremist viewpoints always amaze me. Personally, I think many of these people are mentally challenged. At the very least, they certainly haven't learned how to get their point across. Extremism is also control, which of course is anti-freedom by definition. Every extremist viewpoint includes an amount of control to get its meaning through. Extremism is by and large nothing but control, bringing to the subject many other "isms."

I like to listen to extreme points of view to know where to set the end post. Extreme viewpoints are an excellent example for smarter people to use as a basis for in-depth knowledge of both sides of an issue. You can always start by knowing the extreme viewpoint is wrong for the good of all.

There will always be the extreme "Black or White" factions within any issue. But as we often find out too late, *nothing* is black and white. Those that see it only in one extreme way don't have the good of everyone in mind... or maybe they do intend only the best, but are limited in their forethought. Our freedoms as Americans will hopefully and ultimately get in their way... as was intended.

Because extremists never win, are a bore to listen to, and are usually just shutting their mouths for a second to breathe or wait for the next time they get to speak, we can negate anything they think or say as contributing to a solution. Maybe as end posts within the framework of the discussion as places too far one way or the other, examples of areas not to get close to.

Example:
To get rid of all guns is just as much nonsense as to allow everyone to have one.

Neither of these ideas are viable solutions from any angle at this point in time and both are extreme viewpoints.

We could start from these ends, and move toward the center, considering both of those as end posts. Seems easy, Thank You extremists, you've set our framework in place.

So, to start on this quest for solutions we will negate the jackboot and cordon off the pansy peddlers. No Ghandis, no Hitlers and consequently this means no Torah, no Bible and no Koran also... no religion. ... Imagine.

"You may say I'm a dreamer, but I'm not the only one..."

We have to maintain our collective ego as a people not to be taken lightly with a stern reverence for humanity.

In fact someone we've hopefully all heard of, once said / quoted something similar.

"Walk softly, but carry a big stick." – *Theodore Roosevelt*

Now *that's* an ideal I can personally stand behind.

What we can't have, and can no longer stand for, is the blatant and senseless taking of useful, viable life by those without moral compass or mental capacity. We can all understand how diminished mental capacity reacts in our society, but the definitions of our morals is where we become stuck. Morals are defined by cultural anomalies and are subject to change, even breaking, if one moral overshadows another more dear. Herein lies the American conundrum of life, and its current stumbling block to advancement.

Americans now have no definable morals that aren't for sale and free for the defining as circumstance (money) dictates.

We may have in-fact, stumbled upon a way of life and a form of government these past couple hundred years, to which its only purpose in history will be to display another angle of human failure for future humans to heed.
There is no telling where Capitalism will take us, we've never before been there. Anybody that says they know, hopes to soon have their hand in your pocket. All we can know, is where it has taken us. We can't know where Democracy will end up in our American circumstance, because every day we wake up is new broken ground. We can't look to the past for solid answers because there are no similar situations to look back on. Our current world environment has absolutely no relation to issues of the past. Looking back in history for complete answers is futile. The best we can hope for, is to hold our current situations up to the framework of an overall moral good, and go from there. To try and keep from killing each other as a starting point would be nice. Americans killing Americans is not good, but by itself is apparently not a good enough ideal to take hold.

Part of our Democratic mindset, says that it's ok to separate ourselves into different factions of Americans. To maintain our Capitalist hierarchy, we must separate ourselves. Blacks, whites, yellows and reds. Haves, have-nots and have nothings. Red or Blue, the devil is in the differences. The glue that binds us and the explosives that blow us apart.

One thing that must happen is for all sides of the discussion to agree on the fact that ALL Americans are pronounced to benefit from the United States Constitution. Not Republicans or Democrats, not blacks or whites, not haves or have-nots.

No Amendment can render the main document null.

Our founding Fathers could never have imagined a circumstance in America, where the Second Amendment begins to nullify the Declaration of Independence, and further, the body of the Constitution, in striving for the ideals we had previously declared.

If we are paying attention, we must also contribute to America in some way. Our Contribution isn't in paying our taxes. Taxes are what it takes to live, same as our monthly expenses. You are expected to contribute as you can in other ways, it is a minimum expectation and a place of solidarity we can all start from.

How many people in the U.S. today contribute to their country's well-being or even their country in general? Via our Capitalist attitude we now think that we contribute to our country and are afforded our rights because we pay taxes (give money). We imagine all our freedoms will be maintained without personal investment as long as we pay taxes. We can become armchair politicians to be reckoned with because we are taxed so heavily. It is Materialism and Capitalism that has lulled us into this imaginary entitlement. I would submit that a person or corporation that gives a million dollars a year to the American tax base but works their hardest to maintain cheap labor in other countries while dismissing U.S. labor as too expensive, in fact contributes nothing of substance to the United States.

In fact, that million dollars of tax money is of no consequence at all. They've done nothing to help America but give the government more money to waste, at their own lobbyist's call no doubt.

But with all of this out in the open, we do have an American moral compass to always look upon. One we seem to always forget in lieu of ourselves. It's been defined for us already.

Life, Liberty and the Pursuit of Happiness, an ideal born of Patriots, intended for Patriots… but wait… Patriots?

Boom! I think we can work our way up on the subject through Patriotism. Not necessarily a strict Military style, but social programs for everyone that instill values of Patriotism as Americans above profit. It would help to bring us together and help to quell the separatist movements across the country.

~

Hopefully, somewhere in the previous pages of this chapter I've laid a basis for which we could all hope to come to a modern consensus on issues pertaining to guns in America.

- Adhere to a framework of debate, concession and compromise.
- No extreme actions or viewpoints considered.
- Ideas must maintain America's collective ego.
- Ideas good for ALL within America exercising intellectual morality.

We have all come this far, and this is as far as we go without real answers that don't include depending solely on legislation. Answers that address the core reasons of these problems, the attitudes of people and the reasons they have those attitudes.

Unfortunately, we have been beat to the punch by other "lesser," countries. Countries that we would at first claim as Communist, Socialist or any other "ist" that fits our greedy purpose. Rogue Governments and Countries run by Dictators. Third world back-ass countries, like Canada and Australia.

Let's not worry about Canada, since they have a definite French streak tainting their otherwise exemplary habits, (said in jest) and take a look at the penal colonies of Australia.
A body of land in many ways not un-like our own, and in many ways exactly like our own.

What we DON'T, want to happen here in the United States, is what happened in Australia when bad people with guns pushed too far, and things finally blew up for them.
If a person wants to be even half smart about exploring any subject, then the first thing to do is look around yourself and seek out similar circumstance. There is no more similar circumstance to our own than what happened in 1996 in Australia, this was a mere 24 years ago. We should all know exactly, the what and whys of their entire gun situation and take heed. *What* happened, and *Why* it happened. Their government similarities, the effects during and after. We should explore it ALL, then pull out what we can use. What is the good, and the bad, as it might apply to us and our own conundrum of similar circumstance?

Again, we can all explore further by getting on the internet to get up to speed on Australia's sweeping 1996 gun legislation. I won't go into the nuances here, but I will tell you a couple of the finer points you'll find if you go over it from the start to *finish*.

You'll find that they had similar mass shootings and horrific occurrences, culminating in sweeping gun restrictions, as well as owner and use restrictions. You'll find Australia had a couple well placed Patriots in their ranks. That their structure of government made it a bit easier to pass legislation. You'll also find that Australia is now a much safer place both statistically and personally. Current polls in that country, show the Australian opposition attitude on these restrictions has faded in favor of the ultra-low gun violence rates.

By-the-way, all of this, and there are still legal guns in Australia, but their rules are very restrictive, we can do better.

Their entire situation is a great example for Americans in both terms of what to do and why, and also, what not to do and why. We should be dissecting every nuance of their situation for our own benefit. *They also have a great legislative districting program we should be looking at.* Hint, hint
Something that was not done in Australia that we need to do here to maintain our collective rights as Americans is to;

BREED PATRIOTISM and INSTILL TRAINING.

We have a right to guns that the Australians didn't have. Ours is written within our historic documents, a piece of us as a country, it is our entitlement as well as our bane.

First, we need to... *gulp*... somehow re-visit Patriotism. We need Patriotism in its purest sense. In the sense that we regret we "have but one life to give." The word "Patriot" has been marred by our capitalist culture to sell us things and create control. We need people that aren't swayed by money, see the big picture for Americans, are willing to die politically to see the cause through. Oh yeah, and can keep from being killed or are willing to be martyred before its end. We need a reason to care other than our own individual concerns. We have a couple generations now that have no idea what Patriotism *really* is or what their country affords them as special and why. It's all taken for granted as we try to buy our self-esteem. We can instill an amount of self-esteem in our country via Patriotism.

We will never get past this until we take ourselves out of it and think of others, and that is what Patriotism is about. We have created a complete society strictly against this practice. The capitalist "Me" attitude is very hard to overcome for many people. The only cure for this shallow trap, is knowledge and enlightenment of the world around us and... solidarity.

Unfortunately, in this respect we aren't an American values-based society anymore. We have become a conglomeration of selfish intent surrounded by others of our creation, in a free-for-all fashion. America being merely the name on the fence.

- *Compulsory Service* -

A tactic that changes attitudes and would breed American Patriotism, as well responsibility, and respect for others, is to enlist the service of every able-bodied American teen that can stand it.

In today's technological world environment, each country's ground-based armies are needed less and less for foreign service. We should transition entire divisions of our Army to public Militia service, melding with the National Guard and /or public service-oriented entities. Maybe a mandatory course in high school. Maybe summer programs and training courses. Maybe taking EVERY teen with no place to go, no matter their background. If you have no job or school, you go to the military as a two-year requirement for service to your country.
I would personally like to see a mandatory two-year enlistment for every American teenager no matter what their future plans or education. Say, maybe from eighteen to twenty years old. These two years could be used to instill patriotism, *weapons and defense training*, continuing education, social skills, life skills etc. There is another ancillary effect I can think of to this compulsory service idea. Imagine what kind of street crime, drug abuse and obesity, a plan like this could snub out. All as benefits of looking for ways to curb gun violence. This kind of a program could start to change the United States for the better within five years, probably less. As we already know, knowledge is power, and with it, hopefully the ability to use that power wisely. This knowledge can be taught, and we would all benefit, as a country, from the power realized.

Things to be taught could include gun training with iron clad ideas and definitions such as;

"That force which one knows or should know, can or will cause great personal injury or death and is to be used only in the defense of your life or others, or when charged, in the defense of these United States."

This is the definition of Deadly Force as presented by the United States military. It changes a little, branch to branch, and to add specifics for nuclear weapons etc., but this is the core verbiage. All U.S. Military personnel that get weapons training, must have this or similar memorized.

If the question were to be presented, I would guess that very few American gun owners (less than 20%) would know that there was such a definition, military or not. Shouldn't a person that owns a firearm know some kind of definition of what the law allows, and under which circumstance? Wouldn't /shouldn't the members of a *well-regulated* militia know some definition, word for word? I think that a militia in any sense of the word under any circumstance should.

Shouldn't a well-regulated militia as mentioned in our Second Amendment be adequately trained in some way?

Shouldn't a well-regulated militia be screened in some way? Shouldn't our government know what kind of competent fire power we have at the ready in case our Militia / National Guard is called up?

Yes, it only makes sense.

Patriotism is for your country, not your bunker.

On a side note to this topic... Something strange I've heard used as an argument is that the "Militia" isn't for defense from invading foreign hordes *anymore,* but for when our own government comes to kill us or take our guns. This seems a very skewed take on the original intentions of James Madison.

"Then we will rise up and defend ourselves with our guns to retain our right to bear arms." (seriously, I've heard this several times) That does not seem like a cogent point of view, it just does not seem very well thought out. I can't believe that anyone would say such things out loud, but they do. Basically, this train of thought is a manifesto for suicide.
We are a very "lucky" people as whole. The United States is the only country in the world with such lax gun laws. The way things are going, we are on the road to losing these rights if we don't amend them for the safety of our current culture. Soon the bad among us will lose them for all of us. We are going to have to give up a little to save ourselves and future American gun ownership as a whole. It is an un-fortunate Bottom Line.

But of-course we can never forget that good intentions are meaningless, up to and beyond zilch with no funding.
EVERYTHING TAKES MONEY, every damn little thing.
We must also agree that any changes we make must first pay for themselves or be funded before implementation. Then, next, any source of funding be primarily and forever dedicated to maintenance, improvement or expansion of these changes.
Maybe an instituted ceiling but no raiding the coffers.
Never, None.

You know what might make this argument light up with promise? This whole argument of Yay vs. Nay might get off the ground with a couple ideas.

I have a couple ideas off the top of my head.

A little cheese to go with the whine... so to speak.

* We could charge an entrance fee for visitors to cross our borders, Land, Sea and Air. $25 a head isn't too much, sliding scales for reasons etc. Maybe even tag American travelers for another Lincoln... more or less. We already do that? Do it again.

Boom! Several million a year. Sorry if it makes it a bit more expensive to visit the best country on earth but we have needs and I'm sure foreigners would like a safer country to visit. Here's another that I'd pay to see,

* Violence in all its forms is a luxury. *We like violence, we don't need violence.* A luxury tax on all violence-oriented products would hit the spot nicely.

- Toy guns from likenesses to air rifles
- Violent Video Games
- Real Guns and gun related products
- Violent movies
- Live violence such as wrestling and fighting

Pretty much tax anything and everything having to do with violence at the user end. Same as we did with tobacco products when we decided they were too dangerous but still within our rights to use.

Boom! This would be a major funding source worth billions. So much so that I'm sure it would soon be under attack to be tapped from other angles. We must be diligent in our elected representation to keep our interests in the face of such large amounts of money. Our representatives currently try to spend it on earmark programs for themselves, or to line their own pockets. This would need a lot of oversight.

* Another I can think of is to make offenders help pay for these costs. We could add mandatory fines at all levels of criminal violent offense from misdemeanor on up.

Boom! Several million a year.

Those are my three ideas, now *you* come up with some. Where can we get money from? ... How about from the NRA? We could talk them into the angle of getting out ahead of the problem. Ha! I doubt anyone could sell them on the idea of forethought.

Besides, there's more money in obstruction right now. Change that and the NRA will follow.
*How about requiring gun manufacturers to fund mandatory, high-quality knowledge and training programs so we heavily taxed Americans don't have to pay for it? Hmmm...

Ok, next I'll float a few ideas for possible firearm owner rules. **Not** gun restrictions, *owner rules and restrictions*. No sane and intelligent person would give a gun to anyone standing in a crowd merely because of where they were born. If you would, I'm sorry, this is no longer a viable reason for even ourselves.

Don't forget that we need to be able to keep track of guns to maintain liability and keep them out of the wrong hands and we must abide by the twenty-seven words.
I'll put them over there on their own page again to keep them close for reference.

**"A well regulated militia, being necessary to
the security of a free state, the right
of the people to keep and bear arms
shall not be infringed."**

Ready, Set, Go....

#1 All firearms in the United States must be registered.

- I will submit with a clear conscience, that no person has a right to privacy considering owning a purposeful killing device from the standpoint of public safety. Registering firearms will help us to ensure the owner's liability, ease the government burden to pay for destruction caused by guns, and eventually help with crime in that we can trace movement and use. We already register and trace drugs, cars, explosives etc., in the name of public safety. No one person or group of person's rights for material items is greater than any one person's life. Period.
- No this won't stop illegal firearms. The people who have them now will have them then. Keeping track of serial numbers does not infringe the right to own one. Nor does it cause any more privacy concerns than are already present in modern American life.

#2 No private sales of firearms without legal registered transfer.

- This stands to reason, and is an extension of the idea, of all firearms in America being registered.
- Again, this does not infringe the right to own one. Registration merely helps to keep track of owner's liability in the event it is used wrongfully. Gun stores would benefit from rules such as these, being the natural place for these transfers to take place.

#3 No firearms can be willed after death.

- All guns can transfer legally within the family if the receiving party is legally able. Otherwise, they must be legally sold with the proceeds going to the estate, or be turned in. This stands to reason with the idea of all firearms in America being registered. Again, this does not infringe the right to own one, it merely helps to keep track of owner's liability.

#4 All firearms must be insured for liability.

- This is a major concern with firearms in the United States. There is no cogent argument to not have a killing machine insured against death or injury. Every other blatantly dangerous thing in our lives is insured. More people win than lose when mandatory firearm insurance happens, including every taxpayer in the country and the insurance industry. If nothing else happens, this should be a priority.

#5 Every firearm purchase includes a mandatory gun training and safety course for the type purchased.

- Everyone needs training to do anything adequately in a safe manner. This is on the verge of being a no-brainer. Waived with proof of previous adequate training. All but token costs should be subsidized by Government funding.

#6 All firearms not being used or carried on person by permit, must be locked when not in use.

- It seems common sense to me, and will help to bolster the gun products aftermarket. Also, most likely a requirement under an insurance policy. This idea is a major stumbling block for many people. The argument that a gun needs to be at-the-ready is based in a reality for gun owners so a carry permit or having it in your control at all times could be an answer. Any other firearms not in use should be adequately locked.

#7 All firearm purchases must include a means to secure the gun, such as a trigger lock or safe.

- This goes hand in hand with #6 and encourages safe storage. Many gun companies already include locks and bars with their firearms.

#8 Bi-annual gun buy-back programs.

- Initially there will be a certain number of firearms turned in and each subsequent time will not get as many, but it's not about how many or which type, it's about getting unwanted guns off the streets and removing the potential. The same ones that wind up unattended and stolen or misused. Old and even archaic firearms are still dangerous.

#9 Every firearm purchase includes some type of mandatory Mental Health Evaluation. Every time.

- It is ignorant to initiate programs that depend on mentally ill people or their friends and family to self-diagnose and voluntarily give up their rights or claim the mental disease stigma as their own. We can't depend on families and individuals to self-diagnose and of course this won't stop all mentally ill people. At the very least, it is due diligence on the subject. All but token costs should be subsidized by Government funding.

#10 If a crime is committed with another persons gun, the owner of the gun is held criminally responsible.

- If you can't keep control of your killing device then you bear some responsibility for the outcome if misused by someone else. These aren't toys and need to be as secure as possible. This idea helps put responsibility where it belongs. We have a personal responsibility to everyone else around us not to put each other in danger by leaving dangerous items unattended.

#11 Every firearm purchase includes a mandatory gun violence and defense course. Every other purchase.

- This could include many different aspects and should be thought of as drills for those with guns to keep them sharp and the mind on the subject. All but token costs should be subsidized by Government funding.

#12 Amend years of manufacture for background check for sale to include all types of guns using cartridge ammunition.

- Although not designed for modern charges, many early cartridge guns will accept and fire modern readily available cartridges until they break.

~

There... *Whew!*
That's plenty to swallow, and more than enough ideas on rules from me. I'm sure I've made hit lists from one end to the other with a couple of these pointed suggestions, but like them or not, some of them are even viable. If we in-fact do end up considering rules of any kind or creating lists of firearm serial numbers, whether it be for insurance or government tracking, there would need to be regulations for these things also.
At a minimum I would say that no person or entity should be able to use the rules of U.S. gun ownership to deny access for reasons other than stated in the rules themselves. Meaning that any of these rules can't be used against Americans as punishment for any other infraction or used as basis for inclusion or exclusion or used as a deciding factor in any other circumstance.
And of course, if it should ever come to pass, the roles of registered gun owners should be secured and used for nothing more than criminal apprehension and statistical analysis. This database should be as secure as every other we have and fall under the same acts of privacy statutes as other lists compiled by the government in which we all are already included.

Personally, I don't see the reasoning and correlation between owning a firearm and a need for privacy from the fact of owning that firearm. I am aware of the conspiracy angles concerning this but at the core of the argument... does the government knowing you own a .38 special infringe your right to own it?

Now it's off to thinking about finding ways to rule out other proven dangerous or inadequate minds.
Yes, I'm looking for ways to weed people out, people that are potentially dangerous with a gun by virtue of previous actions. After all, the best indication of future actions are previous actions. As time rolls on, the tighter restrictions on ownership may even help to spur responsibility and restraint as we begin to understand what is at risk.

- Lose the right of gun ownership if discharged from the Military under a dishonorable, or other than honorable conditions discharge.

- Lose the right of gun ownership if you are cited for purposefully using a firearm illegally.

- Lose the right of gun ownership if you are caught with an illegal firearm.

- Lose the right of gun ownership if you purposefully break or conspire to break, any of the rules governing gun ownership.

- Lose the right of gun ownership if you become a confirmed alcoholic.

- Lose the right of gun ownership if you become a confirmed drug addict.

- All people deemed mentally unstable lose the right of gun ownership.

Some of these disqualifiers are personal choices made by people that perhaps could be changed before the bad decisions were made if there were such strict and finite consequences attached.

Is there room for tighter laws and penalties? That itself is another in-depth topic, but in my opinion, there would be plenty of room when only violent offenders are jailed. All others should live out of jail in other monitored programs. nuf-said.

As far as penalties go, I fail, understandably I think, to the strict side of the issue. An Individual's personal responsibility should be a large part of the concern. Conform to the good of all or be cast out. I would not be against strict and finite sentencing requirements such as;

- Mandatory fifteen-year sentence added if crime committed with a gun. All crime across the board. Mandatory sentences double on second offense.

- Mandatory minimum of twenty-five years if anyone killed or maimed with a gun while committing crime. Mandatory life sentence on second offense.

I've left out certain favorite hot topic points such as capacity limits on guns, on purpose. Some think it makes a difference whether a gun holds six shells or fifteen but I don't think it necessarily does. I will concede that it makes a difference at this point in time in the number of dead or injured if a high capacity weapon is used wrongly.

But if we can keep that weapon from being used wrongly in the first place, we should be ok with high capacity weapons. If you think it does make a difference, then use it as one of your own ideas. I don't want to be standing out here alone talking to myself... get on board.

As its own point, I would also take any mention of guns and suicide off the table. Although an alarmingly large number of suicides are committed with a gun, to me it seems a waste of time and effort to muddle the gun owner argument with such a topic. If someone wants to actually take their own life, *as opposed to reaching out for help by feigning suicide,* then how they do it makes no difference. If they have the intent, removing a gun may not help. It is everyone's right to live and die as they please or by which ends they bring. This is a hard pill to swallow, but laws or not, it makes no difference with the final decision does it? We can't pretend to be able to stop suicide at the gun level, this is a mental health issue. It may be better to start looking at *why* so many Americans come to the end of their rope, and take issue with those reasons. Those reasons yes, but also a hard look at why in the "greatest country on earth," we don't care if people kill themselves, by whatever means. We hardly address it at all.

Perhaps the attention to our mental states as we clear hurdles to buy guns, as we are guided through firearms training and as we pay more attention to this issue nationally will weed out some of the terminally distraught, thereby lowering the suicide number by catching the situation early before it ends in disaster.
It is the same situation for suicide as for any other gun use, the gun does not shoot itself. We need to take care of the person, not focus on the tool of the act.
Still, those that use someone else's gun for the deed are a group that we need insurance from. Who pays when an unlocked gun is taken for either a failed or realized suicide?

There will be a lot of people that negate these lists. But I submit that if you are legal, sane, and care in any way about your country, you shouldn't have a problem with at least thinking about doing your part for gun safety and tolerance on this subject. Shootings would definitely go way down, and pride in gun ownership and competent ability would go way up. I'll lay odds that the amount of money quashed in the gun industry from any or all of these ideas would be offset by the expansion, competition and entrepreneurial spirit brought on by the same.

Nothing in these ideas restricts gun ownership by competent Americans. Money and cost of gun ownership has always been there. Everything gets more expensive as time moves forward, we all know that. But I do agree that these costs should be held to a minimum where Government requirements are involved. These previous ideas merely address who the gun owner is and the basic responsibilities a human must realize to own a mechanical killing device of this type in the modern age. Everyone righteous still gets to have a gun or a dozen. We would just now be required to be responsible with our guns and liable for our actions. Yes, we now have to re-define "Righteous" ownership of guns beyond the Second Amendment to adjust for our current population and world environment. The Second Amendment is not the final word and end-all for guns, but guns can be the final end-all for you and your family.
Nothing here even stains or mars the intent of the Second Amendment. These ideas merely create further definition for Americans safety in our modern times. If we can't stomach this change or negate the Second Amendment then perhaps we should once again amend our Constitution, in the name of public safety for all Americans.

If so-called, "Constitutional purists," want to yell and call themselves a "well-regulated militia," let's regulate. If having the world's most powerful military doesn't satisfy your need for protection, then this is all part of regulating our militia.

We have an obligation to a "Well Regulated Militia," so let's get to it, let's regulate the hell out of it. Let's get all American gun owners together by registration to be the patriotic and well-regulated militia that was intended. A veritable force to be reckoned with, Second Amendment says so. That's what the Second Amendment is about, Patriotism and Solidarity in protecting ourselves from outside aggressors as free Americans.

It would be nice if we could forego military schooling and death threats for all our citizens on one end, and riding unicorns over rainbows on the other, for concessions to our habits that would enable us to keep our core rights of gun ownership for long into the future while at the same time bolstering the safety of our population.

Of-course, Obstruction will immediately begin with the hawk of privacy issues. These people won't call themselves obstructionists of course. Generally, they will be waving a flag with an extreme agenda well paid for by some corporate lobbying group. The simple and rational answer to these arguments is that the same people have driver's licenses, passports and insurance policies on the rest of their lives, so insinuating that this particular list of serial numbers would be the list to put us over the edge to final Government oppression is a pretty lame argument. Also, how can one person's privacy trump another person's life under any circumstance? Think about someone in your immediate family being randomly killed. Would "Second Amendment," be enough of an answer for you?

So without falling back on the inane excuses and reasoning that stop at 240+ yr. old velum, what could the reason be?
What reason could a Sane, Law Abiding Patriot citizen of the United States have for saying no to screening gun owners?
Not guns... **Owners.**
The answer to that question lies in the definitions of "Sane," "Law abiding" and "Patriot" and the definitions of these words play with roots in human self-esteem.

If we start now, we can instill enough self-esteem into our children for this issue to be solved in 15-20 years. Yeah, the long run, no instant gratification for us this time. Doing something for our country's future and our children's future, Patriot stuff.

Let's take a look at the terms "Law Abiding", "Patriot" and "Sane," for a minute.

When we speak of "Insane" people, these are not people we can mentally relate to. As you read earlier in this book, I also have extensive personal experience with this issue. There are others in my life, now and previously, besides my first wife, that I haven't mentioned, that would also qualify for this closer scrutiny. People with negative mental issues do things for reasons we cannot comprehend, they do things that don't seem rational. Not being able to understand these actions and strange thought patterns proves us sane at a certain level. Once a person has gone over the edge to an insane state, coming back to normality is generally, not a realistic proposition. The individual's mental condition may be managed with medications, but the propensity for mayhem is constantly present. Truly, insane people aren't as violent or bent on killing as one might think. If and when it comes down to it, I'd say insane people don't care what they kill you with if that is their intent, a knife will do just fine. Over all I would expect most insane people to be pro-gun though. It seems to go hand in hand doesn't it?...
"Crazy People Wielding a Gun! AAaahh!"... Right? ....No.
Without the hype, the real issue with mentally ill people and guns, is just simply keeping them from buying guns and keeping other people's guns away from them, a pro-active situation. Will they hurt themselves or lose, or have it stolen through in-attention? Will they heed gun rules / regulations consistently?

When we talk about "Law Abiding," everyone will claim to be law abiding to your face, but what about in their clique? In their basement?

All humans, no matter where they live on earth, decide which rules and laws to bide of their own individual experience. In America, our privacy rights give us a freedom to cheat our own laws at our individual discretion for reasons of personal want and perceived need. We don't have to tell anyone anything. If we don't like a law, we may not follow it.

Don't get the wrong idea, nobody wants to know what's inside anything of yours you don't want opened, but there is no negating the fact that no matter how many we take off the streets, there will always be illegal weapons. All you have to do is saw the barrel short on an otherwise legal shotgun and you have made an illegal weapon. There will always be those out there, but these numbers will drop over the years to "acceptable," levels with owner regulation, human attrition, and border security.

As far as Patriots go, I challenge you to point to a true modern-day American Patriot.

When we think of what a true American Patriot is, first we should look at the actual definition and see if it matches what we have in our heads. Before Utah, I saw the definition of Patriot differently than I do now.

I was twelve years old in 1976 during America's Bi-Centennial. The "Patriotic" images and talk offered up during our 200th year celebration stuck in my head as a basis for what I had always thought the word patriot represented. This imaging even stuck with me through my years in the Navy, I saw myself within those images. Before Utah, Patriotism was a drummer, a piper and an American flag bearer walking in step with fireworks exploding in their background, there was no question. It meant a minuteman dressed in everyday clothes of the 1700's rushing forward, clutching his rifle, answering his call to arms to thwart the English, I saw no anguish. It meant Betsy Ross wearing a bonnet, rocking in her chair, sewing flag after American flag, I saw no pain or strife associated with this imagery.

Patriotism meant hand over heart, practicing the National Anthem in grade school. It meant baseball, hot dogs, apple pie and Chevrolet.
I had no idea of the meaning of Patriotism other than what was presented to me as a means to incite a celebratory nationalist fervor, or to sell me things. Patriotism was fun, and made me ponder how great it was, that as an American, I was able to buy each American dream as it was presented to me.

But that's not really Patriotism, not even close.

After Utah I have a much better idea of what Patriotism really means. Through my life experience and further investigation, I have found that the word Patriotism is somewhat malleable as to which situations we can apply it to as we claim this word's value in our American culture. But the core meaning, is solidarity of intent for the American cause of intellectual morality, and the willingness, at all cost, to protect that cause.
Meaning it is not about myself, it's about other people.

Those minutemen didn't rush forward for themselves.
If you have ever faced an enemy for your country that was intent on killing you, know that your intention of killing them or willingness to die trying isn't solely to get yourself home in one piece, it's for those that stand behind you. It's for your family, your friends and the people you don't know in your country of all colors and creeds that are depending on you to maintain their right to have their American Dream. You are willing to give up yours so that they, and those that follow can have theirs. You aren't being urged to fight and die by your Government, you are doing your patriotic duty to maintain your Government.
Patriotism walks hand-in-hand with intellectual Morality. In America, a Patriot is doing their duty for black people and Native American people and first-generation immigrants as well as for people like themselves.

Patriotism is not for any personal ideas of injustice someone may hold, but to maintain American ideals of intellectual morality.

But... as far as I can tell, we have no more American Patriots. Flying a flag, attending the 4th of July fireworks show or placing your hand over heart for the countries anthem at a baseball game is not a measure of patriotism. You aren't a Patriot because you will only drive an American car or buy American products. These are all *displays* of patriotism.
Have you noticed that we have also, somehow attached firearms to the word Patriot? I think it's that minuteman visage that has been placed in our heads.
A Patriot is someone of *action,* dedicated to their cause, in this case our American cause. Guns have been a tool for Patriots in the past as we separated ourselves from foreign influence and aggression but firearms aren't actually involved, or needed in today's domestic definition of Patriot. We used them as a tool to maintain our patriotic duties back in the 1700's but under no definition from any angle is a gun included in the definition of the word Patriot.

We have plenty of representatives in our Government and others standing *(many times with guns)* amongst us, that claim to be American Patriots. After-all, they are wearing American flag lapel pins. They were elected in a Democratic vote. They wave a flag. They are now asked questions about our country and cast their representative votes in a chamber with history steeped in patriotism, they must be Patriots, right?

Color me critical, but I am willing to listen to their claims and put them on the list, if they can pass muster by definition. I'm sorry, but very few of our so-called Patriots will be able to come anywhere close in our day and age.
Let's use the following list as core, minimum defining attributes creating a measure for modern Patriotism, also considering money and fear of death...

-   Displays and encourages American core Values.
-   Devotes a part of their life to public service.
-   Has not and does not purposefully use their public office for personal gain, being completely ethical and altruistic.
-   Devoted to Life, Liberty, and the Pursuit of Happiness based in the realities of current America.
-   Does not follow the wants of self, but the needs of many.
-   Would martyr themselves, or their position, for American cause.
-   Can pass a 10 year Personal bank and tax audit.

... Yeah, that's right. From what we see of our current leaders, the very next thing to the exact left of impossible.

But there are people out there on earth within our current generation that strive to meet these goals at acceptable levels of worth within our society.
We have the Pope. This guy is the end-all for his flock. He would definitely fit the framework of being a Patriot for his cause.
Doesn't really help us with our issue here though.
We have Former President Jimmy Carter. He would definitely fit the bill if we could find a way to use his genius before he's gone.
He's a bit too far left for most people though. I think most of us are waiting to call upon his wisdom posthumously.
From here, I'm lost. I'm not really looking, but from the people that are being presented, and from what I'm seeing, I don't think I'm finding a long list of current American Patriots.
We do have a lot of people sitting in Patriot chairs though.

I think that after going over this Patriot angle, it would be good to go over what is *currently* happening to help curb our gun violence epidemic. Maybe take a break from the struggle and look at the lighter side.

What is currently going on and who is doing it? What solutions are currently being tried?

By now, you probably have the idea that I am down on our Government, that I abhor big business and that people suck.

No... not really. I'm just acutely aware of the shortcomings in thought that control how each of these interact in modern America. I'm real tough on the firearms issue and how we are dealing with it, but other than that, I really appreciate our representative's efforts and how our government works.

As far as people go... I know that every American, as all humans do, spend a lot of time in their lives looking for a secure feeling of love. It just scrambles my thoughts to know that somehow, we collectively think we can kill our way there.

People control our Government, people control our business' and people control their own lives. Once again it comes down to people. People don't suck. Americans aren't fools or bloodthirsty Neanderthals. We don't want people dead so that we can have our way. Mob mentality and pots of gold aside, people are trying to do the right thing on several fronts.

Our legislators are stuck between a rock and a hard place, I understand that, we should all understand that and try to help them. The rock being the Second Amendment, and the hard place being the far right and the money they present. When your hands are tied and money is offered up to ease the burden, need softens. They are trying gun and accessory bans. Those are seen as legitimate efforts, but as we have discussed, those will never work to stop the killing. Those are short sighted attempts brought forward in an understandably manic fashion to appease the far left. Some may even pass and be implemented but will be used by the far right as proof of the slippery slope theory. A paradox of intent negated.

A few actions that are being pushed back and forth are Universal background checks and red flag laws. We all need to get on board with these ideas, these are people solutions. These won't stop personal sales but it will stop the ease with which nefarious people can obtain guns at gun shows. We righteous Americans can give up that small bit to help can't we?

Something I've been following lately are the actions of thoughtful people at the heads of large corporations taking responsibility. Yes, the supplier does bear some responsibility for products they sell, and the use of those products, from guns to drugs to high fructose corn syrup. All purveyors of items that can create negative effects on humans, animals and the earth bear a responsibility. From the maker, to the seller, to the user.

I get very excited for our future, and get a very warm feeling of satisfaction when I hear that companies like Dick's Sporting Goods and Wal-Mart are willing to place people over profits and take action. Please support them and buy your goods at companies like these wherever you find them. Show these companies that their efforts are worth it. Help change the dynamic of the American business model to include that responsibility can be profitable.
Conversely, those that stand by and rake in the cash from negative actions of the products they sell, need a second look as to whether we need to do business with them. Be a discerning American, ignore negative examples, think about the results of your actions on your countrymen... *this is a Patriotic action.*

From previous actions, it seems impossible, but money is even getting on board. Did you realize that money is a business? It is, and it is a BIG business. I'm so glad that big money is taking notice. It's hard to pin down how the money industry is included in our gun issue until the angle is brought up for consideration. If any industry can say that they are removed from this subject by customer free will and choice, one would think of the money industry as first on the list if it's included at all. After-all, money is innocuous isn't it? Until we check the angles...
Mass shooters have to buy their guns. One small, yet large block in the road that doesn't hurt anyone is for the money industry to monitor sales and create algorithms to set off alarms when a person buys more than one gun at a time with a credit card.

We have found that several of our past mass shooters didn't have the up-front money to buy their tools so they used credit cards. When anyone buys cases of ammunition or any guns in conjunction with a bullet proof vest or accessory associated with mass shootings, bells can jingle. This practice will get out and people will start using cash to buy their guns and Ammo. GREAT!! Shooters with no money will still have to find another way, or answer questions. One avenue closed-ish.
I've heard word of credit card and bank debit card issuers putting limitations on firearm purchases with their cards and sellers not accepting credit cards for firearm, ammunition and accessory purchases.

It makes me crack a smile. It feels like a roll is on.
Leaders are leading and people are taking charge of their lives. When we finally learn that we've been led into this, and we take charge, life has no choice but to change for the better.
The stiff opposition will temper advancement in other areas, but the roll is on to squeeze thought into this discussion. We should all notice this action happening around us and get on board to help mold an appropriate middle ground.

There are three sides in this discussion, our American Government, including the Constitution, Big Corporate Interest, including money, and the People within the United States.
When "We the People," do come to the inevitable realization that we need, or can allow a little change, *what then?*
We ride our Senators and Congressmen to make the intellectually moral choice of moving towards the middle for the public safety of all Americans.
Or, replace them with those that will. We do the same to the Corporations that stand on both sides of the issue. Those that are conscious and take positive actions deserve our business. Those that stand blindly behind money should feel the sting of lower profits if that's all that matters to them.
And... *we should take personal action.*

Personal action like searching out topical gatherings. Going to Town Hall meetings. Listening and absorbing rather than blocking and deflecting, learning from others. Maybe find an action group and join in. (a list is in the back of the book.) Personal action like being mindful of all that we have talked about here. Mindful and critical of our representation and capitalist system. We need to be thoughtful of other people's ways and means. Thoughtful of as far into the future as we can imagine, and altruistic with our own time and effort in whatever way we can.

We need Patriotism.

- Understanding and Purveyance

This is the most important part. People's attentions are being held by fear. We Americans are dulled to the results of our actions until our own phone rings, until something happens to us personally. We need to deeply understand our situation and then be able to attract or make others aware also. Start discussions with your neighbors and family about guns and your expectations of safety. When your children have sleep overs, ask the hosting parent about guns in their house then follow through with a lite, smiley and factful conversation about guns.
There are many ways we can draw similarities to this situation from life all around us or from previous situation in our own lives. There are solutions by example everywhere that if we take as parable, seem to be a common circumstance from other angles to which we might understand or help others to understand. This following situation is one I experienced first hand...

... A blind curve on a five-lane road.

Everyone in town knows that a lot of people walk across this road at the unseen side of the curve. There are speed limit warning and pedestrian crossing signs and warning signs for the vehicles to slow down and enter the curve with caution at a reduced speed.

The pedestrians walking across have the expectation that any drivers traversing the curve will be adequately cautious with all of these warnings but they seldom are. In fact there have been many incidents in this area where pedestrians are hurt or killed by vehicles piloted by inattentive or non-caring drivers careening around the curve without heeding the signs.
So what do humans do to protect themselves and their children from these uncaring drivers? They take action and put up a cross walk, blinking lights and a speed camera. Any driver now faces vehicular homicide if they kill someone here but everyone still gets to drive their car... and walk safely across the street.

Every person that reads this will hopefully glean its meaning as a simplified version of the bigger picture on our topic here. Once you start thinking about it, you'll notice similar circumstance in metaphor all around you.
Something else to consider when discussing these issues would be to know why our law enforcement agencies and most war zone military personnel are pro-owner control. The people that use guns as a tool in their daily life could most likely bring insight to the table. Over-all I have found these people to not only be pro people control, but pro gun-control also. These people's job includes seeing the wages of free-gun humanity every day of the year. They have training on weaponry and knowledge of the results others don't have... They know what's going on in the trenches of our gun-bloated society and why reductions in fervor and actual competent firearm training is actually needed.

Sometimes we do things, or act certain ways, when we've already had good examples to follow that show the error in these ways.

For instance, a man of many examples...
What happened to our favorite ex-Vice President Dick Cheney's strict no rainbows ideals when he had to face the reality that one of his children was gay? He had to face that issue and learn about things that were actually different than he imagined them to be.

How many gung-ho soldiers have changed their attitudes towards guns when they came home crippled from firefights? What about the second-generation Americans that have been vehemently opposed to immigration reform but find themselves victims of crime by illegal aliens?
The point here is, that when the issue comes to *your* home to roost in a physical way, when you actually get to experience what you've imagined to be one way and it turns out to be different than you imagined, your perception of the issue will change. There really is no choice.

As I mentioned before, with every shooting, with every dead or maimed gun violence statistic, come ten other people turned against guns at some level. Friends and family that have now been confronted with the actual reality of gun violence, think of things and come to conclusions, depending on which side of the topic they stand. With the numbers of shootings in America these days, and the steady increase, we could just wait till everyone has been touched to make a choice. Do we want this choice to be thrust upon us with a horrific phone call?

I can almost hear people thinking to themselves right now.
"... and when that time comes, I'll change."

I know, I know;
I'm just asking everyone to think deeply when the subject arises... and be ready.

~

I'm going to switch gears now to a more aggressive flavor. Let's talk action, not just ideas that we must wait for others to act on. How about a little public dissent?

Public dissent itself is not a solution, that is true. What public dissent does, is to call attention to the subject and help keep this issue in the front of people's minds after the news cycle ends.

These previously presented ideas for solutions, although powerful on their own, are for wall flowers and pacifists. *(yes, you are being a pacifist if you sit by and let all this happen around you and take no action.).* Those things take time to implement, public dissent urges them forward.

Throughout this book I have been urging thought on action, consequence, and change. Many thoughtful people do this, we see them on talk shows, news broadcasts and on bookshelves. These call-outs come from both the right and the left in one form or another.

But still... we have no real action. Why is that?

After pondering this situation, I've come to the conclusion that everyday American people are not the only people afraid of the things that we have discussed here. Somehow, we see our country's representatives and the upper echelons of our country as untouchables. When was the last time a well-insulated American was the target of random gun violence? When was the last time a very wealthy person or government official was killed in a drive-by shooting?

I felt a blip, a kind of Matrix stutter step, when James Hodgkinson shot U.S. House Majority Whip Steve Scalise, U.S. Capitol Police officer Crystal Griner, Congressional aide Zack Barth, and lobbyist Matt Mika back in 2017 at the Congressional baseball game. *(what were lobbyists doing there?)* Their usual heavy security failed them that day. Generally, these people aren't actually out in the public realm, and when they are, it is with heavy security, translated; *No urgency.*

We are discussing gun owners and their attitudes. We are discussing non-gun owners and their attitudes. The way these attitudes are presented to us is via murder and destruction. Plain and simple, no matter which side of the firearms issue you are on, you are afraid of guns. No matter which echelon of society you claim, you are afraid of guns. Anyone who says they aren't is a liar, or probably hasn't thought too deeply on the subject.

I am more than sure, no, I am positive, that money plays a large part in our representative's decision making when taking no positive action but there is a darker reason. A reason that few will admit to on camera or recording. A reason they fear will make them look even more weak as they don't act.

Our representatives, although well insulated aren't immune, or martyr material. They are afraid to take action because THEY are afraid of guns and the people that own them. THEY are afraid that either themselves or their family members will be targeted for death if they challenge the people that love guns. They are afraid they will be run out of office and the futures of their families might be at stake. If there is no more gun lobby money to pad their lives, what will they do?

In short, *if that were the case,* they would be a bunch of cowards sitting in Patriot seats.

Not a claim, just a thought.

Well guess what... I am no longer afraid of guns or death. I am willing to stand up and champion this cause in the face of guns. I am willing to stand up for the good, honest, loving and hard-working Americans that are threatened day in and day out in "the greatest country on earth." I am willing to do more than write a book and collect accolades while hiding myself away. But I'm not running for office, just up on a soap box. A lot of us are tired of bowing to people spewing selfish thoughts. Tired of people threatening with numbers and money... and guns

I live very simply now and need very little money to survive. I've seen the end of life and I am ok with it coming again.

I perceive that my family has come to the conclusion that the changes that occurred in me after my shooting will most likely not end. They were there when the phone rang. Their hearts broke under the weight of what, at the time, seemed to be the end of Mike. They experienced, and now are more sensitive to what I am saying here. I think they can understand my point, and now realize the gravity of murder in the family.

Why not use my experience to help those that I will eventually leave behind?

This Solution?

STAND UP AND YELL

Tell that person walking around with a gun on their belt that you don't appreciate it. Confront them at whatever level you are comfortable with. Of course, make sure they aren't authorized officially or as a requirement, be discerning. Keep your emotions in check. Calmly talk to, and confront them, without harassment or violence.

Here is an example of a situation I've had before:

"I don't want to upset you or anything, but I'll tell you, I don't appreciate that. You need to conceal that thing."
"What? It's my right to wear my gun anywhere I want."
I know that, I'm just saying it's not safe.

Then I turned away as he threw a few choice words at me.
Do I think this was effective? No, not to the dude wearing the gun, but to the dozen or so people that saw, I'd say yes, they had no choice but to think.
Does confrontation sound crazy? *It isn't if you are serious.* People that are on the short list to death every day as they merely go about their business should be serious about this.
If you see open carry in a store, if you are opposed, it's a good idea to find the manager and tell them you don't appreciate it.
If anyone ever pulls a gun out inappropriately or threatens you with a gun any way, call the police and press charges. If you follow through and they are convicted of improper use, they can lose their right of gun ownership. Then walk away without looking back. The last thing we need are hotheads with a gun walking around. Us hotheads without a gun are bad enough. This topic *does* warm my ears, but a person needs to keep their emotions in check when they are wearing a gun, that's the rule.

Also, I don't know how many times I've seen open carried handguns sitting in holsters as easy picking. Guys with an armful of stuff skirting through the aisles of Wal-Mart with their .45's dangling precariously from an un-strapped holster. *(I've never seen open-carry in Nordstrom or Dillards)* When you are in possession of a firearm, your mind is on the firearm at all times, especially when in public. How close will a State Patrol Officer let you get to them?
Not close enough to get their gun.
For some, it is hard to imagine, for others, it is just part of life.

That's why we need to, **STAND UP AND YELL.**

Demand out loud that your representatives stop avoiding town hall meetings. Call their offices and leave a pointed message. When a town hall meeting comes up anywhere in your area, gather others and attend. Calmly and firmly turn all town hall meetings into referendums on people with guns. When or if the attending representative shrinks and withdraws, FIRE THEM and make sure they know why. Maybe they are cowards and money-grubbing opportunist that need to be replaced. Tell them that their opportunity to pad their retirements is finished. Remind them;
In the end, we will remember not the words of our enemies, but the silence of our friends and trustees.
You may recognize this last sentence as something you have heard before, I hope so. It is paraphrased from a Martin Luther King Speech, but I added a couple words for the cause. A gun may have killed Dr. King but it could not kill his message. Another, in-our-face, testament to the effectiveness of guns being an answer to solve personal ideologic issues, they can't. We must put our emotions aside, *and we must think.*

STAND UP AND YELL

Call your Representatives offices and demand they do something. DO NOT shrink, DO NOT stop until there is positive action taken.

TALK to your friends and family about this issue. Prepare yourself and what you will say. Don't just jump in without a plan. Tell them you love them and don't want to see them die. Bring it home, ask them what they would do if they got that call about you. Tell them this issue is the most important issue we as Americans face in today's world. Tell them that LOVE conquers all, not guns. Love is not just a religious ideal, it is what we all strive to feel no matter our views on life.

BE A PAIN IN THE ASS

Don't let this issue fade away until the next shooting that you *hear of* on tv. Arm yourself with the facts but pull them from a large bag of love and understanding for those around you. Make this a daily conversation not to be shunned. Make people think about this whether they want to or not. Remind them that no action, is action in the opposite direction. If you aren't part of the solution, you are part of the problem.

Righteous indignation is *my* mantra, make it yours or we will all inevitably suffer the consequences.

If not now... When?
When the phone rings? When you go to identify the body? After the funeral? From the afterlife?

Do you need help? Do you need even more motivation? email me at the address provided at the end of this book. I will be glad to show up, provide books, champion your cause and comfort and counsel the grieving.

American Druthers

- What do you Think? -

Everything written here is a bit of my personal experience of the world. This is all *my* point of view. A seldom heard point of view, from the receiving end. All stemming from a little patient observation, a bit of needed action, and now, being forced by this very topic, a lot in-depth thinking.

As you might imagine, I have a lot of time to think.

I'm thinking that ever since waking up a day or so later from being killed and revived to the life I have now, I have been suffering an indignation. I sit here writing this book seven years after the fact of my own shooting and this indignation has not waned. There is no indignation in being shot by a murderous and maniacal drug fiend, but there is for the position I have been put in by the American system and politics surrounding the gun issue here in America. I am a well vested American. And now, after being shot, nothing more than a pain in the ass to everyone in the big picture, on both sides of the American firearm topic. The kind that stirs the pot and makes you uncomfortable no matter what your position on the subject.

I draw attentions that seem to always end with a sour twinge. Maybe you think I should sit down and shut up, suck it up and fade away... sorry, but that's not going to happen, Hell No. I still have family and countrymen in actual need.

Now, when I am in a crowd of new friends my injuries will soon become too much for the curious and invariably someone will ask the question, *"if you don't mind may I ask..."*

Sometimes I'll laugh it off with a pithy or humorous reply such as "I cut myself shaving" or "Bowling accident," something as ridiculous as that.

These evasive type answers work both ways, sometimes the curious folks stop there with a chuckle thinking they may have gone too far and then become uncomfortable, sometimes not. Either way it goes, the party gets crashed.

If I'm in a mood for conversation and just give it to them straight, many people seem genuinely horrified. Some will search for an obtuse reason and excuse themselves. Sometimes I see things behind people's eyes that disturb me. Grown men with white beards look at me like I'm their Mother and I've just scolded them. Everyone is immediately sure I'm at the very least an anti-gun zealot now, if not some kind of fanatic writing down names and taking notes. If not overtly anti-gun then certainly by my obvious proxy, a walking, talking admonishment to their lifestyle. Someone who has lived the truth behind their favorite subject and doesn't like it. This makes a lot of the evening's conversations uncomfortable, even though I offer nothing they imagine much. Soon I have to hold back the urge to condescend. Violence is always a close topic in some form, and it seems a bit too close for comfort with me in certain company.

I try to stay out of the way, or quell the rising tension, but once everyone knows exactly the circumstance, just by people seeing me getting around occasionally, it reminds them of the gun issues all around them. In person is too much, on TV is enough.

Even though it makes a lot of people uncomfortable, this is of course most hazardous to the ideas on the pro-gun side of the issue. Usually, and in short time I am distanced from people in the gun crowd, mainly because I lived.

For instance; I had a previous "friend" in St. George Utah that went as far as to tell me it was my fault I got shot because I occasionally smoked pot, I brought it on myself. *(don't pretend you're shocked, I am a child of the 70's after-all)* His argument being that in his world, my attacker being on meth when he shot me somehow correlates. Another was adamant that I should have been holding a gun or had one within easy reach at all times.

Hmmm. For a while, those two idjits made my ears turn red. But let me tell you this; As someone that believes in, and still lives the ideals of :

"We Hold these Truths to be Self Evident"
"Life, Liberty and the Pursuit of Happiness"
and   "ALL Men Are Created Equal"

Whether I own a gun or not, I will not sit around anywhere in my life and have a gun purposefully within reach. That takes away my Liberty by putting restriction on my life and makes me sad to think that others actually do this. What a paranoid waste of life. Is this what we have been reduced to?
No sir, I'm going to live my life with no guns from now on.
I don't feel that I'm here on earth to kill or be killed. What kind of life is it to have to depend on a gun for your self-worth? It is small minded and selfish attitudes like these that are hard to understand until you actually know the person holding them dear and can see the reasons why they are so scared in their lives. It's obvious to everyone that knows those previous friends of mine why they are such twits. They give plenty of excuses for bad behavior and need guns to maintain their self-esteem and they get manic when the firearm topic comes up. If those two choose a gun over a good friend, Good Riddance I say.

If I would have died it would have been just fine. If I would have died, I would have ended up just another number in a statistics table in the spring of the following year and nobody would have to be bothered. My pro-gun friends would have remembered me in reverence and then postulated on how they would have eviscerated my attacker with their weapons and what I did wrong to cause my own end. The anti-gun folks would have pulled me from the statistics to use me as a martyr for their cause. I'm glad I didn't die though, if merely for the singular reason that I won't become a statistic for either side of the issue to claim.

Neither side wants a statistic that thinks and talks. That's one of the underlying reasons we don't hear much about the yearly injury number. But I'm not all knowing, I don't know what exactly to say or do in this circumstance, I take it as it comes and deal with attitudes and short-sighted thought accordingly. What I did do with little or no choice was to face this issue daily. In the mirror is one way to face it, but if I was *really* serious, I could move to the most overtly gun fanatical town in the country and stare it in the eye every single day, two or three times a day. I could immerse myself in a microcosm of real and imagined gun violence that I've since learned has sent many over the edge, yet attracted many more.

Yes, I was serious. That's what I did.

Soon after being discharged from the hospital and recouping for a month at close family's house in Las Vegas, I somewhat crazily moved to a small and sleepy little town that kept guns in the front of my mind. Not to whine of my infirmity, but for importance in my new train of thought. A town where literally more than half the people you see are packing heat and there is a gunfight at least three times a day, every day, No Lie.

(A riddle. *Where in America is there such a town?*)

I moved to a town where the gun attitude is up front, and will slap you harder than being pistol whipped. Many people carry their pistols on their hip like nobody's business, and it's not, this is America. Everywhere you might go, even in the surrounding county, there are guns out in the open at all times…. a way to keep the love story alive.

No, I'm not crazy now. I consider my time in that little burg as facing the demon and a continuance, of penance to be paid. Besides, it did kind of grow on me, the climate is nice and there's not actually *much* gun violence, just a lot of bravado both real and imagined. Certainly 100% more than in most every other town its size in America, but manageable enough to excuse with a paranoid American mindset.

This itself is an interesting fact to note. The gun play, and
bravado displayed in that town, is actually NOT a pro-gun
argument "realized," as many on the fence might think.
It is actually just the opposite for that particular town.
The idea being; lower gun violence and theft if everyone is
wearing a gun because doers of bad will think twice in the face of
guns everywhere. That town has blatant theft like all others and
someone is shot or killed there quite often in comparison to all
other small towns of its size.
The actual truth is that other than suicide, there is little or no gun
violence in every small rural town in the entire United States,
whether there are guns present or not.
Why is that?
The short answer, is that in a small town, everyone knows each
other. The long answer has to do with the desensitizing effects of
guns everywhere and the complacency we all experience within
this environment.

While traveling around the country with my son, I would write
an article or two, here and there, for Blogs or Magazines on the
experiences we had. That turned out well and even paid a little.
It's nice to have extra gas money to supplement the retirement
fund but it was nothing anyone could live on. I was able to write
about what I knew and someone appreciated it. I've tried to do
the same here and hope a few people in America will take notice
and appreciate it also.
What a lot of people seem to miss in todays "me, me, me, gotta
have it now" society is the fact that nothing good or worthwhile
comes easy, free, or right away. We have become used to this as a
sales technique to sell us things, but this issue of guns and the
people that use them is just too engrained for immediate
gratification. We are going to have to pay a little special attention
to this issue either now or later.
It is true, owner screening won't take all the illegal guns off the
streets immediately.

But over a few years, the illegal and unregistered guns will float to the surface until one day there won't be a large number out there. We aren't a stupid society, but sometimes we forget, it's about our future, not our immediate gratification.

There is something that makes me sad about my own experience. Those people that know me, and know exactly what happened to me, *(conditions and all)* then took it as a reason to buy more guns or start carrying a gun around on a daily basis. It saddens me to think that my experience has made anyone more paranoid. This is the opposite of what should be the case. It is the opposite of what I personally want for all my friends, and family, and the people around me at all times. I would like everyone to stop the paranoia, feel safe and loved.
No need to fear guns. No need for guns...

...Yeah, I'm not betting on that.
The only way that could happen is if people stopped being afraid of each other, or if there were no guns around.
Fat chance huh?

Well, that's pretty much it... except...
Did the dedication in this book stir you up at all?
Did you even see it, or read it all the way through?
No need to turn back,

With Love, and Hope for a better future, this book is dedicated to the families and friends of those killed or maimed in U.S. Sanctioned Gun Violence within the borders of our Free American Society.

There it is again...
As I sit here on the couch, myself crippled from American gun violence, I want to remind everyone reading this book what this "nonsense," is really all about.

This is about ALL Americans and their loved ones
This is about YOUR children
This is about YOUR friends and family
This is about maintaining YOUR gun rights

Some might think it sounds a bit extreme to classify what happens here in the United States every day with a word as stern as "sanctioned."

Sanction, is one of those great English words that can support two opposite meanings. You can restrict with sanction and you can allow with sanction. At this point in America's history, gun violence is effectively a government sanctioned event. If we don't take action to stop the shootings, we are allowing it.

To those people that are incredulous about this subject, I respond with resounding clarity...

...What you haven't done, is what you have done.

- The End -

Postscript:

Here is where I'm going to put ideas that don't really have a place, or fit directly into the text of the book.

It is important to be very strict on this issue, but light hearted prodding is always fun. There is a recently older movie (from the 1990's) that takes on our government's political payola issues. There is very little mention of the gun issue, it's more about the Lobby Industry. It is a sage message as well as being a hoot. I recommend the movie "Bullworth" to those interested.

For anyone that wants to see the entirety of the coverage covering my own incident, this link will take you to a page at the St. George Newspaper online. The top part of the page will have today's news and all the tagged stories involving my case are below. https://www.stgeorgeutah.com/news/archive/tag/craig-manwill-bennett/

The "sleepy little town," mentioned in the last chapter was/is Tombstone, Arizona.
I'd like to thank everyone in Tombstone for putting up with that strange guy limping through town in Cabana Wear for a year and a half. It was a real stretch of my mind when one of the few friends I met there was shot dead in the street during my stay. I'd like to thank Leroy and his memory as a bit of common sense that was worth more than a "walkdown" to that town.
Also, I must thank my Very Best Friend in Tombstone. It was in her adobe duplex that I conquered my demons.
Thank You So Much Nickel. Your help meant everything to me.

Does that surprise anyone?
I mean that I, being a victim, also knew another victim. Guess what, I know a couple others also. My Mother in-law's employer in Seattle was shot for her car keys in a car-jacking incident.
I am so sorry for Gloria's husband and children.... soooo sorry.

A friend of mine I met on the road previous to myself being shot caught some "pepper" *(a stray bullet)* in the desert and suffered permanent nerve damage from the results.
I know a woman, the widow of a now deceased friend, that experienced one of her children being shot and killed here in America. Muriel knows what this is about.
Help Save America's Families from this.
These are the reasons....

To be an American.... "American." What does that word mean to you? As I think about it, it seems to fall in ranks with the words Gun, Freedom and Love, something different to everyone that hears it. Invoking feelings others may not feel, for reasons some will kill you for, but sometimes, no-one cares.
For wants of self and needs of current comforts.
For much of Americas life, being an American held a feeling of belonging. Being an American enveloped our lives. The world is so small now and thought has followed in kind to the point that a small screen held in our hands can now hold our attentions above all else. Our attentions are being held primarily for money to the detriment of our American lives.
In today's world it would be a sad thing to be able to point out that someone could have avoided the carnage if they were only paying attention to their environment rather than their phone. I'm not aware of any specific circumstance although I'm sure that has happened.

Something I've learned in my experience is that there are only two ways to die. No matter how we get there, our end will come. How we have lived our lives getting to the end is where our death will take us. As a living organism, we humans start our decline in our thirties, about the same time most have set their lives trajectory.
Even though; There are only two paths to death, two ways to die. Fighting Love and Love.

We will spend our lives in a **_never-ending_** battle against Love, which is a very hard battle, never to be won. Or we will strive to live a life of love. The ultimate test of a human life, the hardest battle to fight, a box of a thousand crosses, a path so hard to walk, few even dare.

The most satisfying life to lead.

Peace only comes with love, there is no other way. Humans cannot kill for peace, it is impossible. This is an idea that helps to perpetuate our gun culture and it is completely false. Guns have not brought us security, they have brought us death, destruction and more guns.

The last thing I can think of for this book and its post script is actually a question.

Who will go down in history as our Greatest American Patriot?

Let's not have the people we love die by the gun.

What do you think?
How about giving some feedback?

sanegunsforamerica@gmail.com

or

americandruthers.blogspot.com

Common Sense Action Organizations

Moms Demand Action -
>   https://momsdemandaction.org

The Coalition to Stop Gun Violence -
>   https://www.csgv.org

Giffords Law Center to Prevent Gun Violence -
>   https://lawcenter.giffords.org

March for Our Lives -
>   https://marchforourlives.com

Brady United Against Gun Violence -
>   https://www.bradyunited.org

**Look for other books of interest by
Michael McNaney**

Made in the USA
Columbia, SC
12 August 2020

15005392R00117